"The work of Dr. Chow is _____ _____ _____ of _____ Healing Arts is truly symboli_____ _____ _____ Western orthodox medicine wi_____ _____ _____ [BRARY has had remarkable success _____ _____ _____ EVARD significance is the fact that Dr. _____ _____ system subjected to scientific validation."

> Dr. Thomas Malone
> Former Deputy Director
> National Institutes of Health

"Dr. Chow radiates such positive energy she seems as tall as the tallest building. I have gained more from my sessions with her than from any other branch of holistic medicine."

> Nev Munro, Ex Olympic Athlete,
> Lawyer, and Author of *Exiled to Parkinson's Disease*

"Last summer I was having trouble with my hip joint and it was aggravating. Every time I walked it bothered me. You (Dr. Chow) did some manipulation around my knee and my hip was transformed! You have the strongest hands I have ever felt."

> Bill Good, CKNW Radio
> Vancouver, British Columbia, Canada

"Qigong is indeed a healing miracle and this dynamic book is required reading for anyone who wants to experience the benefits from it."

> Christopher Hegarty
> President, International Center
> for Life Improvement

"I feel 100% better physically, emotionally, and mentally. Thank you."

> Hilda Harris
> Renowned opera singer

"A great majority of our people said your presentation was the best motivational talk they've ever heard. Our San Francisco agency just completed its most successful campaign in our history. Thank you (Dr. Chow) for helping us find our peak performance."

William Quiring, C.L.U.
General Manager
Prudential Insurance (S.F)

Back cover photo: Master Chow treating Mr. Robert R. Walker, Jr., with emitted qi, who wrote the following:

"My introduction to Dr. Effie Chow occurred when she was brought in to treat my father who had been immobilized by a stroke. Previously, he had spent four months in the hospital going through intensive therapy with no noticeable results. After just one month of working with Dr. Chow, my dad was walking and showed steady improvement.

"Over the past years, I have had Dr. Chow treat my entire family for various illnesses and injuries ranging from hypertension, pinched nerves, various pains, stomach problems, and damaged ligaments. While all ailments showed improvement, there was also significant improvement in the areas that were stress related."

Robert R. Walker, Jr.
President, M.H. Realty Advisors

MIRACLE HEALING FROM CHINA...

QIGONG

MIRACLE HEALING FROM CHINA...
QIGONG

Charles T. McGee, M.D.
with Qigong Master Effie Poy Yew Chow, Ph.D.,
R.N., C.A.

MEDIPRESS

Information in this book is not intended to replace the services of a trained health care professional, or serve as a replacement for medical care. Consult your physician or health care professional before following the authors' proposed courses of exercises. Any application of the methods described in this book is at the reader's discretion and sole risk.

Fourth Printing 1996
Published in the United States by

MEDIPRESS
PO Box 5154
Coeur d'Alene, ID 83814-1952

McGee, Charles T., and Chow, Effie Poy Yew
Miracle Healing From China ...QIGONG

Bibliography: pgs. 256
Includes Index.
1. Health. 2. Traditional Chinese Medicine. 3. Healing.
4. Miracles. 5. Qigong. 6. Chi Kung. 7. New Age.
8. Complementary Medicine. 9. Alternative Medicine. 10. Holistic Medicine.

Library of Congress Number 94-096177

ISBN 0-9636979-5-1

Printed in the United States of America

ACKNOWLEDGEMENTS:

The authors express their sincere gratitude to the following people who made this book possible: Professor Stephen Kong, Ph.D., President and Chairman of Sino-American Medical Technology Communications, International, Beijing, China; Kenneth Sancier, Ph.D., of the Qigong Institute, East West Academy of Healing Arts, San Francisco; Professor Zuyin Lu, of the Institute of High Energy Physics, China Academy of Sciences, Beijing, China; Feng Li-da M.D., Ph.D., Director of the Chinese Immunology Research Center, Beijing, China; Howard Dewar of China Advocates, San Francisco; Qigong Master Yuan Xikui, presently of Montevideo, Uruguay; Dr. Zhao Zuo An, of Harbin, China, for advice and material; Qigong Masters Sun Yun Cai and Liu Hengshun of Beijing, China; Mr. Liu Xiao of the Guo Lin Research Society and husband of Qigong Master Guo Lin; Bill Chao, President of Innovative Systems and Technologies, Inc., of Milpitas, California, for help in assembling materials; Fuller Royal, M.D., for his Kirlian photographs; Barbara Cooper, Martha Zirschky and Pat Rowe for editorial assistance; and to the many unnamed persons, family, friends, and associates who have been of great help and support to us in bringing Medical Qigong and Traditional Chinese Medicine to a position of respect in the Western countries.

TABLE OF CONTENTS

PREFACE

Qigong is an ancient philosophical system of harmonious integration of the human body with the Universe. It is an art and science that plays an active role in protecting and strengthening health, preventing and treating diseases, resisting premature senility, and prolonging life. Qigong has succeeded akin to a miracle where all else has failed. Ancients referred to Qigong as the method to "eliminate diseases and prolong life." Qigong is the modern pinyin spelling, but also is written as Chi Kung, Qi Gong, and Chi Gung, among others. It is pronounced "chee-goong."

Qigong is derived from two words. "Qi" is the term used in Traditional Chinese Medicine for our vital breath, life force or energy. The concept has no direct counterpart in Western culture. It is roughly the equivalent of "bio-energy" (living energy), or electromagnetic energy. This "living energy" is the vital life force that permeates all of nature. It is the force in our bodies that controls our biochemistry and all other functions and behavior.

"Gong" can mean discipline, work, or skill. Therefore, Qigong has been defined roughly as "energy work," and "breath work." It also has been called "air energy" because, through breathing exercises, energy is absorbed from the atmosphere.

This book, co-authored by Dr. McGee and Dr. Chow, is written to introduce Qigong to the general public, not as a text for academia. Qigong is a deep compelling subject, and only a few of its theoretical principles are introduced here. Through examples of case histories and research, we present the full range of health and medical benefits that are possible with Qigong. We hope this will motivate those who do not know of it to explore and practice this fascinating ancient discipline. The text is written primarily in the first person of Dr.

McGee. The Qigong system presented is that developed by Qigong Master Effie Poy Yew Chow, Ph.D., R.N., C.A., and titled The Chow Integrated Healing System (The Chow System).

Some people whose case histories are presented in this book requested anonymity, so their names have been changed. Others wanted to share their phenomenal results with the world, and insisted that their real names be used.

Please write to us about any positive changes or experiences, however small, which may occur with your use of the material in this book. You may remain anonymous if you wish, but we would like the privilege of sharing your experience to inspire others to have hope regardless of the situation. What you may consider to be insignificant may be of utmost importance to others. So, please share with us.

We also invite you to send us any questions or comments you may have. Your feedback will be valuable for our on-going work in helping humanity evolve through a very challenging time to a more healthy, loving, rich, and peaceful life.

INTRODUCTION

"Miracles" in healing are real and now occur so frequently in China they have become commonplace. These "miracles" are the result of the practice of an ancient Chinese discipline known as Qigong.

Qigong is the mother of Traditional Chinese Medicine. Thousands of years old, it remained veiled in secrecy and available only to the elite until the early 1980s. Over the past decade, research in China and elsewhere has documented many unbelievable events, even the complete disappearance of some cancers!

In China more than 70 million people converge in parks every morning to do a graceful-looking exercise in unison. They are practicing Qigong to increase energy levels, feel good, and stay well. They also are motivated by an awareness of the powerful healing potential of Qigong.

Now, Qigong has come to America. Organizations devoted to spreading the practice of Qigong currently are small in number, but are multiplying. Although the number of "Qigong masters" in North America remains small, it is growing. A "Qigong master" is a person who has developed the ability to emit healing energy from the body, and has a certain expertise, long experience, and proven success in healing with qi.

One of these Qigong masters is Effie Poy Yew Chow, Ph.D., R.N., C.A. (certified acupuncturist) of San Francisco, who has been healing with and teaching Qigong for more than thirty years. By integrating Qigong with health supporting measures from the West, Traditional Chinese Medicine, and some of her own original concepts of a holistic approach to a person's body, mind, and spirit, she created her own style of Qigong.

The Chow Integrated Healing System can accelerate the results of Qigong practice, and has been shown to be remarkably effective in a wide range of situations. These include applications in corporate health, sports medicine, post trauma and surgery, conditions associated with the aging process, and chronic diseases which generally are considered to be untreatable. It also has applications in business settings as a means of motivating people to reach peak levels of efficiency and performance.

My purpose in writing this book is to describe the wonderful healing potential of Qigong, and to share Dr. Chow's unique system with you. As a Western trained medical doctor, I was naturally skeptical of the claims of Qigong treatment until I saw, then experienced first hand what it can do. Now, I am convinced that Qigong has great value and deserves to be incorporated into every healing system in the world. It costs very little, seldom is associated with any side effects if learned and practiced properly, and can be applied by anyone, anywhere. It can produce true healing and optimal health, and a wonderful sense of fulfillment.

As you read the book, please consider this: If Qigong can cure cancer and facilitate healing in cerebral palsy and other serious diseases, imagine its limitless potential in the promotion of health and in the cure of less serious conditions.

Chapter 1: QIGONG IN ACTION

"The philosophies of one age have become the absurdities of the next, and the foolishness of yesterday has become the wisdom of tomorrow."

Sir William Osler
Montreal Medical Journal, 1902

RECOVERY FROM CEREBRAL PALSY

Eight year old Eric had been crippled by cerebral palsy since birth. After two short hours with Qigong Master Effie Chow, he was able to walk and run normally, and not fall on his face. How could this be?

It is a terrible tragedy to be born with cerebral palsy. Victims of this disease sometimes compare it to a life sentence in prison, without the possibility of parole. They are born with a mind that thinks and feels normally, but is trapped in a body they can't control. They move with jerky, uncoordinated movements, and their speech often is unintelligible. Western medicine says that the condition is permanent, and offers no hope.

For all of his eight years, Eric suffered from many of the problems associated with cerebral palsy. Most noticeable were deformities of his left hand and foot, as well as poor coordination. He had been receiving physical therapy at a major neurological institute and hospital in British Columbia since he was two years old.

The fingers of Eric's left hand were flexed in a permanently contracted position and could not be forced open. It was extremely difficult, or impossible, for him to perform the most common tasks with the hand.

The Achilles tendon on Eric's left leg was short, which prevented normal movements of his ankle. The contracted tendon pulled the foot down so far that the top of his foot and shin formed a straight line. Even his physical therapists were unable to forcibly flex his foot upward from this position. Eric had to walk on the toes of his foot which produced an awkward dipping to the right. Anytime he increased his pace, his body was thrust forward, throwing him flat on his face. In addition, as his speed increased, his left arm would contract and jerk uncontrollably.

Eric's doctors had already performed one surgical procedure to lengthen the Achilles tendon, but it had failed. A second operation was planned: the prospects for improvement were not good. His parents had been told he would never get better.

Dr. Effie Chow was invited to the medical facility in 1987 by a Home Nurses Association to present a weekend seminar in what announcements referred to as Energy and Touch Healing. As is usual in these seminars, a difficult patient was selected by the hospital staff to participate in a healing demonstration. Eric's physical therapists nominated him to be the test patient. His parents, though separated, were together that weekend to support their son in any way possible.

The seventy-five health professionals who attended the demonstration had no idea what to expect. They certainly had not come expecting to witness what we in the West would call a miracle. Dr. Chow's expectations were open-ended. Her intent was to teach the professionals and parents what could be done with Eric. She encouraged everyone to note changes if any occurred. She was fully open to noticeable improvements; things the audience couldn't imagine--healings the Western medical system considers to be impossible.

Eric and Dr. Chow met. She engaged him in some "let's get-to-know-each other" talk. His rehabilitation doctor and physical therapist were at his side to give moral support and to observe the procedure closely. After establishing herself as a friend, she asked him to sit on the table and tell everyone what he would wish for if he could have his fondest dream granted. Dr. Chow says she has discovered through the years that people need more reasons to recover from an illness than simply wanting to recover.

Eric's eyes became brighter as he told her he dreamed of riding a skateboard and also of kicking a soccer ball, things he had never been able to do. He aspired to more than simply kicking a ball. He wanted to kick it *better* than his friends. As Eric described his dreams, the room became quiet. These were impossible ambitions for a boy who had a difficult time walking.

Dr. Chow began to work with Eric, continuing to converse with him normally. She first concentrated on his deformed hand by placing it in hers and stroking it. She instructed Eric to breathe deeply and sit with good posture. People in the audience had no way of knowing what really was happening; it appeared she was doing nothing more than massaging the hand. Actually, she was using Qigong maneuvers to flood Eric's tissues with an unseen healing force or energy, the mysterious thing known as qi (pronounced "chee").

Within only twenty minutes, the impossible began to occur. Eric's hand and fingers were softening up enough for the audience to see that something highly unusual was happening. Many spectators appeared quite curious. Within twenty minutes all five of Eric's fingers could be extended fully and the hand looked normal. He was able to pick up a large coin with the left hand using only his thumb and forefinger. The therapists had asked Eric to try this immediately before the session, but he could not do so. He had never been able to do this in all of his eight years.

The audience, especially the physical therapists, clapped with joy. They had neither seen nor heard of anything like this before. What they had seen was beyond what was possible in Western medicine, truly qualifying to be called a miracle. However, this was just the beginning.

Dr. Chow switched her attention to Eric's left foot. She first asked Eric's rehabilitation physician to test the ankle one last time to demonstrate its range of motion. As it had been since birth, the ankle was absolutely stiff with the foot extended down as far as it could go.

Once again, the audience watched as she handled his foot with her hands, apparently applying a massage. For several minutes nothing seemed to be happening, but soon the ankle joint relaxed and became more flexible. Dr. Chow continued treating Eric for a full thirty minutes as she tried to explain to the audience what she was doing. She then turned Eric so the audience could see his foot better, and asked his rehabilitation physician to examine the foot. When he did so, he was amazed to find he could push it up to form a ninety degree angle at the ankle. This was the first time in Eric's life that the foot had ever been in this position. Dr. Chow asked Eric to stand up and put all of his weight on his left leg with the foot flat on the floor. When he discovered he could, he smiled broadly.

With a little of coaching, Eric was able to walk around the room with his left foot flat on the floor. This felt so unusual to him he had to be reminded again and again not to walk on his toes.

Dr. Chow encouraged him to quicken his pace. When he did so his left arm moved in a smooth coordinated fashion without jerking. He was able to trot with his left foot landing flat on the floor. This time, to his amazement, he didn't fall forward on his face.

Eric was asked to do a deep knee bend. He flexed down so far his buttocks touched his heels. As he did so, he was able to keep both feet flat on the floor, demonstrating just how flexible his left ankle had become. He had been touched by the miracle of Qigong, and was thrilled. People in the audience understood the odds against what they had seen and many were moved to tears. Eric's parents openly cried tears of joy. Again, everyone applauded and he grinned broadly, proud of what he could do.

Another private treatment was scheduled for the next day. Only Eric's parents and his physical therapists were in attendance. At the end of the session one of the physical therapists brought out a skateboard. Eric approached the skateboard, stepped up on it with one foot, and pushed off. At first he was a bit shaky and needed prompting, but he was at least able to ride the skateboard slowly and carefully.

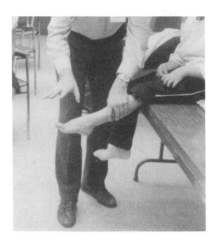

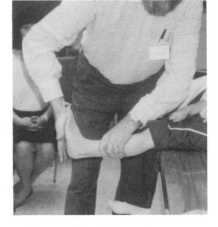

Figure 1. Immobile position of Eric's left foot since birth.

Figure 2. Left foot is flexed to a ninety degree angle by Eric's rehabilitation physician after Qigong therapy by Dr. Chow.

Dr. Chow returned to the center six months later to see how Eric was doing and to give him another treatment. She found that he was maintaining his improvements very well. This was surprising because he was not engaged in any kind of Qigong maintenance program, and had learned nothing about how to practice Qigong. At the completion of the session, a physical therapist offered Eric a cloth ball. He walked up to the ball with confidence and kicked it around the room. All of his wishes had come true and he was ecstatic.

Notes written by Eric's physical therapist before and after these treatment sessions can be found in Appendix I.

CANCER

Feng Jian, a national badminton champion in China, was diagnosed as having lung cancer at the age of twenty-one. His doctors were surprised when Feng refused surgery, chemotherapy, or irradiation treatments. They were even more astonished ten months later when the cancer had vanished. Once again a miraculous cure followed the practice of Qigong.

By the early 1980s most people in China had heard of Qigong. However, few people had attempted to treat anything as serious as cancer with Qigong, and the entire subject was viewed with a high degree of skepticism. People heard tales of miraculous recoveries following Qigong practice, but few believed them.

A news story was aired on national television about the use of Qigong by a well known sports figure. After that single favorable exposure, millions of people began to change their opinion of Qigong. I was told in China that today's widespread practice of Qigong can be dated from this one incident.

There was no doubt about Feng Jian's diagnosis. A large tumor in the left lung showed up on an x-ray, and a tissue examination confirmed it was a cancer. His physicians advised treatment with the usual Western approaches of surgery, followed by irradiation and/or chemotherapy.

Feng rejected this advice and chose to treat himself with Qigong, a highly unusual decision at the time. He began to practice Guo Lin Qigong, a form of walking Qigong, developed by a woman named Guo Lin, who cured herself of advanced cancer of the uterus. This style of Qigong is used specifically in the treatment of cancer.

Feng followed a strict daily pattern that consisted of nothing more than eating, sleeping, and Qigong exercises. He practiced Qigong during every possible waking moment, twelve to fourteen hours per day, seven days a week.

Feng began to feel better within days. Ten months later his x-rays showed some scars, but the cancer had vanished. He is alive and in good health ten years later.

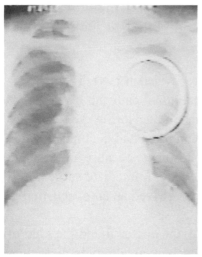

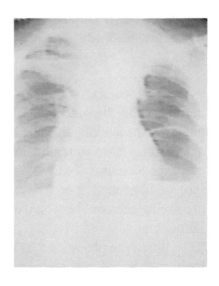

Figure 3. Feng's chest x-ray with a large area of cancer circled. (photos from video tape)

Figure 4. Feng's chest x-ray ten months later. Some scarring remains, but the cancer is gone.

In China, I was shown pictures of Feng's x-rays and a video tape of him practicing Qigong with other cancer victims in a park. The tape also showed him playing ping pong three years after his recovery. He gained more weight than he had lost and appeared to be in excellent health.

This one miraculous recovery had a very positive impact, not only on the public, but on Western trained physicians in China as well. Doctors no longer rejected Qigong automatically every time they heard it mentioned. They began to alter their thinking and were willing to say, "There appears to be something to it." I have heard that phrase from Western trained physicians all over China.

HOPE

Hope was lucky to be alive after emergency surgery. A large cancer had caused a perforation of her small intestine. Facing certain death, she applied healing methods of The Chow System, and is alive and free of cancer thirteen years later.

Hope was sixty-two when she nearly died in 1981. The first sign of trouble was the sudden onset of abdominal pain and fever. At the time she was working in a small village in the Northwest Territories of Canada, a town so remote its hospital often had doctors available only on a temporary basis. Hope was fortunate because an excellent surgeon happened to be available that day. Immediate surgery was life-saving because she would not have survived an air evacuation to Edmonton.

When the abdomen was opened, the doctor found the kind of problem that makes surgeons wish they had gone into dermatology. A large cancer had been growing quietly in her abdomen for some time, measuring eight inches in diameter in its largest area. That particular day it caused some tissue to die and the small bowel developed a leak. Bowel contents were oozing into the abdominal cavity causing a life threatening infection (peritonitis).

Even if infection had not been present, a surgical removal would have been impossible because of the extent of the cancer. The bowel leak was sealed, drains placed, the abdomen closed, and Hope was given huge doses of antibiotics. The diagnosis was fibrosarcoma (Grade II), a form of cancer generally treated with irradiation, but unresponsive to other treatments.

After recuperating for a month, Hope was told she was going to die; she would be lucky if she lived two more years. She was not a candidate for irradiation therapy because of the location of the cancer. In desperation, her doctors recommended a trial of chemotherapy, but told her in advance it probably wouldn't work. Hope started the toxic treatment and experienced the usual side effects of nausea, vomiting, weight loss, and hair loss. Periodic CAT scans were not encouraging. The cancer did shrink a small amount, but after five months of chemotherapy her oncologist wrote in her medical record, "I don't believe chemotherapy will help this lady," and the treatment was stopped.

Hope always had been receptive to alternative approaches. At this point two friends who had taken a 100 hour course from Dr. Chow encouraged her to practice qi balancing exercises centered around Qigong. Hope (her real name and a good name for this story) was looking for something like this to come along, and was receptive. There were many more things she wanted to do in her life, and she didn't want a "little cancer problem" to upset her plans. Hope was a very positive-minded person with a good sense of humor.

She practiced Qigong diligently, along with the other measures described later, and her miracle began to happen. When she began Qigong her abdomen was so swollen with cancer she looked six months pregnant. Over the next four months her abdomen shrank, CAT scans showed a steady reduction in the size of the cancer, and she began to feel like life might be worth living again.

At this point her friends asked what she would like to do more than anything else. She said she wanted to visit with friends at her alma mater in Berkeley, and on the East coast. Not long before, she thought she would never be able to see her old friends again. She took the trip, knowing it would be therapeutic.

When Hope returned to the clinic for a follow up exam, (four months after beginning routines of The Chow System), a CAT scan showed that the original cancer mass had disappeared, but a suspicious mass remained in the left kidney. The kidney was removed surgically, but no evidence of cancer was found.

Hope still had little energy, and was fearful the cancer would return. In October, 1982, she began Dr. Chow's training course to perfect her energy balancing practices, and much more. Classes were spread out over several months, but at the end she felt so much better she was able to go back to work full time.

Thirteen years have now passed since Hope's recovery. She is cancer free and enjoying good health. In contrast to most people who are looking for a quick fix for their health problems, she faithfully practices the exercises that cured her and continue to keep her healthy. She is well aware that she needs to do so to keep the cancer from returning.

I interviewed Hope in 1994. Her current interest is to write a book about her experiences so that others may benefit.

THE MIRACLE OF QIGONG

These three miraculous recoveries are but a few among many (more are described in Chapter 10). Each demonstrates a different way in which the principles of Qigong can be applied.

Eric was treated by Dr. Chow with what is called "emitted qi," but he also learned to practice proper posture and how to breathe with his diaphragm. Feng Jian practiced a style of Qigong that was developed in China specifically for cancer, and practiced diligently on a full time basis, twelve to fourteen hours a day. Hope learned Dr. Chow's healing methods indirectly, practiced diligently every day, and her cancer went away. She regards curing her cancer with techniques she learned second hand to be a high tribute to the power of The Chow System. She continues to practice these measures daily at the age of seventy-five.

Almost anyone can learn to do Qigong and benefit from the practice in some way. The best part about Qigong is that after training, it costs nothing but time, effort, and persistence. Results improve with practice, and the phrase "You get out of it what you put into it" is most appropriate.

Qigong is backed by over a decade of scientific research.

Hundreds of studies have been reported demonstrating that the effects of Qigong energies can be measured on plants, animals, humans, and even inanimate matter. These studies have been carried out in scores of academic institutions of the highest caliber.

Qigong is worthy of your attention. It is an amazing discipline that is new in the West, but beginning to spread rapidly. Qigong practice can produce results that force us to redefine the borderline between the possible and the impossible.

Chapter 2: ORIGINS

"The way to long life and health is quite simple and often escapes the attention of those who look for complicated solutions."
Dai Liu
Daoist Health Exercise Book

In China, Qigong is a household word to hundreds of millions of people. If you ask someone about Qigong, you see a twinkle in the person's eye with the reply, "Oh, you know about Qigong." You get the impression that a special secret is being shared.

If you ask people in the West if they have heard about Qigong, the answer is usually negative, but this is not really true. Most of us have seen pictures of groups of Chinese people practicing Taiji (formerly called Tai Chi Chuan) routines in the morning, and Bruce Lee movies publicizing martial arts to the masses. Both of these disciplines are related to Qigong.

HISTORY OF QIGONG

According to Yuan Xikui, a Qigong master in Beijing who researched the ancient texts for us, a verbal tradition of practices resembling Qigong may go back as far as 10,000 years. Reports describe a dance called Da-Wu (Big Dance) used for celebration ceremonies and religious purposes. Apparently, it was discovered quite early that Da Wu, the ancient precursor to Qigong, could cure some diseases and produce a strong body.

Written records about Qigong date back 4,000 years. A different dance was described which was intended to direct body movements, regulate breathing and qi (our vital life force energy), and heal diseases. Therefore, Qigong predates the development of acupuncture and the martial arts, and is said to be the earliest form of what later developed into Traditional Chinese Medicine (abbreviated as TCM). Through history, Qigong developed into soft (medical) Qigong, and hard (martial arts) Qigong.

In the sixth century B.C., the scholar Laozi suggested a method of health preservation through the regulation of respiration. A contemporary of Laozi wrote, "Inhaling and exhaling helps to rid one of the stale and take in the fresh. Moving as a bear and stretching as a bird can result in longevity." Drawings of body positions in the exercises are preserved in carved girdle pendants of jade that date from that era.

In the second century A.D., Hua Tuo invented a series of Qigong routines called the "Frolics of Five Animals" (Wuqinxi), which imitate the movements of the tiger, deer, bear, monkey, and bird. These animal-like Qigong exercises and their variations are practiced widely today. Fortunately, over 100 ancient books have survived to modern times, providing a long history of Qigong.

Throughout most of the past, Qigong practices were kept secret among intellectuals, the elite, and the privileged. Over time, Qigong exercises and practices were modified or expanded and new ones appeared. Related methods from India and Tibet were incorporated into existing Qigong practices between the first and fifth centuries A.D.

Around the fifth century A.D. martial arts applications of Qigong were discovered. The Shaolin Monastery in Henan province became famous as a leading martial arts center in China. It is more famous to people in the West because of the *Kung Fu* television series and its sequels.

During the seventh century, a group of Chinese physicians compiled a collection of traditional cures from across the country in a classic medical text, *On the Causes and Symptoms of Diseases.* Included were a total of 260 Qigong methods used for treating 110 varieties of illness. Different sources have noted that there may be between 2,000 and 4,000 different styles of Qigong!

Qigong permeates Chinese history, and Emperors frequently

learned how to practice it themselves. Rumor says that the third emperor of the Chin Dynasty killed competitors to his throne (his own brothers) by using a Qigong martial arts technique. Later he was killed by the small daughter of an adversary who sneaked into the Imperial Palace at night and used the same technique on him.

Ancient Chinese warriors learned a martial arts technique called *Steel Body* Qigong. When they entered battle, the weapons of the time didn't cut, burn, or crush them. Dr. Stephen Kong, my host in China, told me that ancient documents report that when a large sword was swung at one of these warriors, its movement was stopped about six inches from the body by the warrior's energy field. When firearms were developed, steel bodied warriors believed they could fend off bullets, but found they could not. At that point their military superiority was lost.

In China, many modern martial arts (hard Qigong) performers earn their living performing feats in public. A high value is placed on these hard Qigong performances, and people gladly pay as much as ten dollars (U.S.) for a ticket, about one-third of a monthly wage for an average worker. They enjoy seeing people do *impossible* feats such as breaking bricks on the head with a sledge hammer, balancing the body on a sharp steel spear, and biting off a piece of red hot steel, then lighting somebody's cigarette with the red hot rod. Though few people would want to develop this aspect of Qigong, it does indicate the level to which human potential can be pushed. The major interest is in soft, or medical Qigong and what it can do to promote health and healing.

Many Qigong exercises have been developed over the past 3,000 to 4,000 years, and new ones continue to be unearthed. Fortunately, for general health purposes, only a few exercises need to be learned. Various exercises are done in lying, sitting, or standing positions. There are both stationary and moving exercises. There are exercises that develop "internal qi" and "external qi."

In China, people may try several different exercises before

selecting those they are able and willing to do on a continual basis. Usually they continue to practice the methods of teachers they admire and from whom they have gained some personal satisfaction.

Taiji is an exercise now popular in the West which developed from Qigong about 900 years ago. Taiji is a useful discipline for maintaining health and energy levels, and has helped control some disease conditions, such as high blood pressure. However, there are more powerful Qigong exercises that produce much stronger healing effects than those of Taiji.

The Shanghai Qigong Research Institute, established in 1953, was the first of its kind anywhere in the world. About that time, a book by Lin Gui-Zhen, *The Practices of Qigong Therapy,* verified that Qigong had a solid basis in science. This led to its more widespread use. By 1959 reports of good results from Qigong treatment were beginning to circulate.

During the Cultural Revolution (1966-1976), the Chinese government suppressed all activities and endeavors that were connected with ancient customs. The open practice of Qigong often led to public harassment and possibly even death at the hands of teen-aged Red Guards, so all Qigong activities went underground. After the end of the Cultural Revolution, Qigong practice came out into the open again. However, critics attacked it as being based on activities and beliefs contrary to governmental policies concerning religious practice and superstition. To resolve the question, the government funded studies to evaluate the essence of Qigong. Qigong was found to have a scientific basis and, in 1979, many hospitals of Traditional Chinese Medicine (TCM) began to offer Qigong as an accepted treatment method.

Since 1982, Qigong research and therapeutic activities have increased, and more Qigong research organizations have been organized. Many TCM hospitals now specialize in Qigong treatment.

THE POTENTIAL OF QIGONG

Qigong is a discipline anyone can learn. Most people practice Qigong simply because it makes them feel good, perform better, experience higher levels of energy and stamina, and reach their level of optimal health. Qigong can improve sports performance, prevent jet lag, and supercharge the immune system. Qigong practice has been shown to super-oxygenate the cells of the body. It can reduce stress, improve bowel function, and relieve the symptoms of insomnia and sleep disorders. In the area of pain control, Qigong practice can relieve acute and chronic pain, reduce the pain of childbirth, and speed recovery from sports or other injuries. In addition, Qigong can increase the effectiveness of Western medications, even allowing the use of smaller doses which may reduce the risk of dangerous side effects.

Qigong has value in the treatment of more serious problems. It can reduce healing time after surgery by 50%, normalize the blood pressure, and heal tuberculosis. It can heal gastric and duodenal ulcers, chronic atrophic gastritis (stomach inflammation), and liver disease. It can relieve nearsightedness (myopia) and improve mental performance. It also has been effective in the treatment of substance abuse, obesity, respiratory conditions, asthma, and allergies.

Benefits have also been seen in a long list of serious neuromuscular conditions, such as post-stroke syndrome, paralysis from brain and spinal cord injuries, multiple sclerosis, aphasia (loss of the power of expression of speech), Parkinson's disease, and cerebral palsy.

In more than thirty research studies Qigong has been found to reverse the effects of aging. Qigong has improved or reversed the results of many medical tests that become abnormal with age. In addition, it has cured many of the diseases that are common to senior citizens.

Qigong has been shown to reduce deaths related to high blood pressure, reduce the frequency of strokes, reduce the incidence of retinopathy (deterioration of the back of the eye), improve the efficiency of the pumping action of the heart, and decrease blood viscosity ("thin" the blood). It also has improved EKG (heart) and EEG (brain) readings, normalized the level of sex hormones, and improved blood sugar levels in diabetics.

A slowing of the aging process is consistent with personal observations. Dr. Chow and I have met many Qigong masters in China and elderly masters routinely look about twenty years younger than their chronological ages. Their cheeks are smooth and shiny. They emit a healthy glow and they have few wrinkles in their skin.

The enhancement of sexual power and treatment of sexual dysfunction with Qigong has a long history. Chinese emperors allegedly learned Qigong techniques that delayed an orgasm, enabling them to have sex with a string of concubines, one after another. Entire books have been written about the application of Qigong in impotency, frigidity, and the improvement of a normal sex life. Some are available in English. Dr. Chow has treated many people successfully for impotency, other sexual dysfunctions, and for enhancing normal sexual qi.

Cancer patients usually benefit from Qigong practice. According to representatives of the Guo Lin Research Society, over one million cancer victims now practice Qigong every day. Their cancers have either stopped growing, shrunk, or disappeared completely.

As mentioned previously, Qigong can reduce or eliminate the side effects from chemotherapy. It also can reduce the need for pain medication, and improve the appetite and sense of well-being in patients with advanced cancer. Terminal cancer patients who practice Qigong usually die with dignity, with little or no pain, have a better quality of life, and feel comfortable right up to the end. Thus they avoid being medicated into a narcotic stupor, a sad and common fate in the West.

It is difficult to determine how effective Qigong might be as a primary treatment for cancer, and research is needed in this area. Only on rare occasions have cancer patients elected to use Qigong as their only therapy. According to Dr. Kong, in China most patients with cancer choose to go to Western hospitals where they begin treatment with conventional Western methods. Cancer victims generally do not try Qigong until the Western methods have failed, the cancer is far advanced, and the chance for a complete cure is slim.

Even in desperate circumstances dramatic changes can be seen in cancer patients. Dr. Pang Heming is a doctor of both Western medicine and TCM and director of the Zhi Neng Qigong Hospital, Shijiazhuang, Hebei province. There are generally about 200 cancer patients in the hospital at any one time. Dr. Pang reports, "We have hundreds of patients practicing (Qigong) together, building up an energy field. We ask people with cancers we can see or feel to stay in the middle of the group. After a session, the cancers shrink, or even disappear. This is real, something valuable."

Though research shows that Qigong can improve health and miraculous cures have been verified, experienced Qigong masters caution it is not a "cure all." There is one major characteristic of Qigong that sets it apart from other tales of miraculous recoveries. Healing benefits from Qigong are the result of the practice of a discipline that involves time, patience, and commitment. If people who benefit from Qigong don't continue to practice the measures that help them, their progress may disappear and they may slip back into their previous problem. They need to practice and/or have treatment until they have built up their internal qi sufficiently to maintain their good health status.

RESEARCH IN QIGONG

Dr. Kenneth Sancier, a chemist and Co-President of the Qigong Institute, East West Academy of Healing Arts, San Francisco, has been diligent in his search and review of the scientific literature supporting Qigong. Dr. Sancier has been a scientist all of his life. He retired from SRI International, a world renown private research institution, after a distinguished career with eleven patents to his name. He reports that since 1986, over 800 scientific papers on Qigong have been presented in a total of eight international conferences.

The "First World Conference for Academic Exchange of Medical Qigong" was held in Beijing in October, 1988, and a second such conference was held in 1993. Hundreds of scientific papers were presented at these conferences, most of them describing research conducted in academic institutions in China. Selected abstracts of these reports can be found in Chapter 8.

I am not aware of any other medical studies comparable to these. Many of the papers report results that sound miraculous. Researchers described the effects of emitted qi on plants, animals, humans, and inanimate matter. For example, physicists described measuring several kinds of physical energies coming from the hands of Qigong masters when they are in the "Qigong state," emitting qi. The wide range of phenomena associated with Qigong is more comprehensive and different from anything previously described in science.

QIGONG APPEARS DECEPTIVELY SIMPLE

When you observe people doing Qigong exercises, it is difficult to comprehend the great potential of a practice that appears so elementary. According to Master Jia Guori, a long time Qigong practitioner and author in China, the method is easy to learn, but too simple to believe. Therefore, people frequently are reluctant to persevere enough in their practice to achieve results.

The most common forms of healing Qigong are do-it-yourself exercises that should be learned from a reliable source. In China, people may practice recommended exercises for variable periods of time on a daily basis. A person who is basically healthy may practice Qigong to improve vitality and an all around sense of well-being, allotting thirty minutes in the morning and an additional thirty minutes in the evening. If a serious disease or illness is involved, people may practice exercises that are specific for their condition five or six hours, or even twelve hours a day, with some breaks in between.

When used as a treatment for serious diseases such as cancer or strokes, Qigong is often used in conjunction with other commonly used modalities. People with cancer may be treated with surgery, chemotherapy at markedly reduced doses, radiation therapy, herbs, acupuncture, and other modalities of TCM.

In stroke patients, Qigong may be combined with acupuncture, herbs, massage therapy, physical therapy and a form of guided imagery. Some patients elect to practice or be treated with Qigong alone, without the use of other treatment modalities. It must be noted that treatments are customized for each particular person. TCM and Qigong work with specific imbalances of qi that are different in individuals, even though people may have been given the same diagnosis in the Western system.

Some Qigong exercises involve slow rhythmic walking, stopping, stretching, and breathing. Practitioners may remain stationary and roll an object similar to a rolling pin in their palms to stimulate specific energy points; make slow side to side movements while uttering low groans; or may stand with legs apart and inhale and exhale in a specific pattern as they put their hands, arms, and body through deliberate movements. There are still, non-moving forms, specific moving forms, and also free-style moving forms.

Breathing generally is done with the diaphragm, as we all once did correctly when we were babies. The mind stays alert, yet relaxed at the same time. Sometimes the mind focuses on a certain body area or energy point while breaths are counted. The mind state may or may not resemble a meditation state, but should be calm. As mentioned previously, there are thousands of Qigong exercises.

Qigong treatment forms vary. The Qigong master may emit qi at a distance or close proximity, and solicit the participation of the patient. When treating with emitted qi, the Qigong master may work on qi imbalances he or she sees, or senses, by passing hands over the patient at some distance from the body. He or she may point wiggling fingers at the patient, may physically apply pressure to certain qi points of the body (acupoint therapy), or touch-heal with different hand movements.

In a stroke patient with contracted limbs, the master may emit balancing energy directly into the tissues involved. The elbow or knee can be tested periodically to see if its range of motion can be increased. It is possible to straighten out a limb that has been contracted for years in only a few seconds. This is an event I would never expect Western physicians to believe unless they saw it first hand as I have.

In Beijing, Master Xia Lei-Ming told me that he can treat patients with emitted qi all day long without becoming fatigued. However, most Qigong masters are unable to do this and treat only four or five people daily because of their own loss of energy. They prefer to emit qi only to patients who are unable to do their own exercises, such as babies and people with severe neurological conditions. After a treatment these masters must perform their own Qigong exercises to return their energy levels to pre-treatment levels.

Like Master Xia, Dr. Chow does not tire while treating, but becomes even more invigorated. She has learned how to replenish her qi while working with patients and has treated as many as nineteen people successively. She shares and teaches this process and its importance to students, particularly in her advanced classes.

Qigong masters may treat patients who are passive in the early stages of treatment. However, they prefer to teach patients how to practice themselves, so that patients will feel the gratification of being in control of their life again and can assume responsibility for their own healing.

Patients who suddenly have been ambulated may require daily treatments for variable amounts of time by a Qigong master for as long as six weeks or more before the frequency can be decreased. After that, patients might be on their own and occasionally be seen by the master for a "tune up." The wise patient will continue to practice the exercises and disciplines that have been effective. In China, most people are pragmatic and disciplined enough to do this.

COMMONLY OBSERVED EFFECTS OF QIGONG AMONG BEGINNERS

Learning Qigong takes time, work, and patience. Some people notice energy sensations in the body almost immediately. Others may require weeks, or even a year or two to notice any changes. It depends upon the sensitivity and openness of the individual. Some effects are highly subjective, and will vary in different people. Objective effects include a clearing of the complexion, increased hair and fingernail growth, regrowth of lost hair, return of hair to its previous color, softer skin, increased alertness, and an increase in physical activity.

People also experience improvement in digestion, a stabilization of weight in the direction needed, increased sex drive, relief of pain, and a softening of old scars. Bowel and bladder functions may improve, as well as sleep patterns, mood, and levels of energy and stamina. Most people who practice Qigong soon find they don't need as many hours of sleep as previously. After a while, the exercises create time for themselves, no longer competing with other activities. In China, hospitalized patients frequently are encouraged to practice Qigong during their recovery period. Most patients report they can feel benefits from the exercises, and continue to practice Qigong long after leaving the hospital.

PRECAUTIONS IN USING QIGONG

Currently, in China, people follow better health habits and quieter and less complicated life styles than in the West, and have different qi disturbances and blocks. Therefore, there are few cases of side effects in China from the practice of Qigong.

In the West, our diets, health habits, and the environment have been declining in quality for over 100 years. Our lives are complicated with multiple levels of problems, spiritual emptiness, emotional and physical stress, violence, anxiety, restrictive diets, chemicals, allergies, over-medication, lack of exercise, and excessive living. Because of this, most of us manifest complex energy blocks and disturbances.

When the practice of Qigong alters qi levels, the complexity of qi blocks and disturbances may be amplified, an undesirable outcome. The difficulties may relate also to the form of Qigong practiced, and tend to occur with the more forceful styles. This problem generally is seen in young people who normally have higher energy levels than older people.

Most Qigong masters who have emigrated from China generally are unaware of these different conditions in the West. Some have been surprised when their students become ill from Qigong practice, and on a few occasions the masters have been unable to bring them back into balance. A small number of masters from China have stopped teaching because of this problem, and now follow the safer occupation of writing.

Several people have come to Dr. Chow to resolve problems that have arisen from other Qigong and touch healing courses. Their symptoms have ranged from migraine headaches to a general sense of not feeling right, and even minor changes in mood. She has had success in treating these people with emitted qi, along with other supportive measures included in The Chow System, helping them rebalance their internal qi.

She has found that if people aren't willing to follow other measures that support health and normal energy balance, it is difficult to clear energy blocks permanently. This is why she stresses that Qigong exercises should be combined with other energy balancing measures, and not practiced by themselves. Therefore, it may not be a good idea to casually pick up a Qigong book and begin to practice whatever style of exercises may be described.

The methods Dr. Chow teaches are gentle and, in her experience, can be practiced by anyone, young or old. In over thirty years she has never seen harm come to anyone who followed her teachings. Some people may have physical limitations in executing the exercises, and other phases of her program, but there are no inherent risks if they make an honest and careful effort.

Therefore, contraindications to Qigong practice may relate to the style of Qigong. If you are learning a style other than the one herein described, you should consult with your instructor about possible risks and complications from the method.

LESSONS FROM A MASTER ARE DESIRABLE

Master Chow stresses that it is always wise to have some personal lessons from a Qigong master, in addition to trying to learn from a book or video. Being in the presence of a Qigong master's qi can be of primary importance in building your own qi and proficiency. Minute perfections of movement, pose, or posture, can make a world of difference in the flow of qi.

I can verify this observation from personal experience. When I took Dr. Chow's 100 hour program there were thirty students in the class. We were learning Qigong exercises in a small group, and assumed we would have little difficulty mimicking her movements and positions. Frequently she asked us to hold certain positions in an exercise while she checked each student. Even in the presence of a master who was patiently detailing what we should do, we continued to make errors which could affect results we hoped to achieve. It was remarkable how a slight alteration of our posture or positioning by Dr. Chow could increase our sense of the flow of qi so much.

Figure 1. Dr. Chow corrects a student's position in an exercise.

Chapter 3: QIGONG MASTER CHOW

"The dramatic effect of Qigong for me has exceeded all expectations. This is the beginning of a new life for me, at age sixty-four."
Stewart Wong, Ph.D., Washington, D.C.

"I was amazed that within ten minutes she (Dr. Chow) had my neck turning, fully mobile. I had been unable to do that since an injury fourteen years previously."
Pat Rowe, R.N., Vancouver, B.C.

Dr. Chow is a powerful healer and the most visible proponent of medical Qigong in the West. For over thirty years she has been working to integrate Traditional Chinese Medicine (TCM) into Western medicine. To achieve this goal, she founded the East West Academy of Healing Arts in 1973. Later, in 1988, an arm of that organization, the Qigong Institute, was founded with Dr. Kenneth Sancier (a chemist and senior research scientist retired from SRI International in Palo Alto, California) to promote research in medical Qigong.

Dr. Chow is the only Qigong master in North America who has been active in the development of health policies within the Department of Health and Human Services (DHHS), and in the field of alternative medicine. For over twenty-five years she has been a consultant with DHHS and the National Institutes of Health (NIH) and has served as an appointed member of the National Advisory Council to The Secretary of DHHS on Health Professions' Education for Medicine, Osteopathy, Dentistry, Veterinary Medicine, Optometry, Pharmacy, and Podiatry (MODVOPP). She was appointed to the Ad Hoc Advisory Panel of the Congress-mandated Office of Alternative Medicine at NIH, Bethesda, Maryland, and to the Scientific Advisory board of the Richard and Hinda Rosenthal Center for Alternative and Complementary Medicine at Columbia

University, New York.

A CHALLENGING CASE

After observing miraculous healing with Qigong in China, I decided to look into Qigong activities in the United States, and it didn't take long to locate Dr. Chow. I decided to verify her claims of being a Qigong master by referring one of my patients to her. I wanted to see if she could produce a miracle in someone I knew.

John had an early cancer of the prostate. I have met few people who were more receptive to alternative healing methods than he. When informed of the diagnosis, he consulted several major medical centers and made dozens of phone calls to explore all of his treatment options. He finally chose to receive x-ray treatment at Stanford University Medical Center.

About fifty percent of men who are treated for prostate cancer become impotent, regardless of whether they have surgery or irradiation. This happened to John, and he had not functioned sexually for over a year. He had flown all over the United States and spent a great deal of money exploring courses of action that might bring back his sex life. John was receptive to my suggestion that he see Dr. Chow and give Qigong a try.

I was in San Francisco on the day of John's first appointment, and met Dr. Chow. She is a cheerful person with a very high energy level. Her attitude seems to say, "Let's get busy with this impossible task and get it done." Everything about her is upbeat and optimistic.

I observed quietly as Master Chow evaluated John, beginning with a routine medical-social history. She showed as much interest in the important events in John's life as she did in his medical problems. She then began to teach John proper posture, how to breathe properly, and a few of her personally selected and modified Qigong exercises. This first visit lasted a full three hours, terminating with an acupuncture treatment.

The next day I met John and his wife for breakfast, and their enthusiasm could not be contained. For the first time in more than a year, John had been able to perform sexually.

DR. CHOW'S EARLY LIFE

Dr. Chow's family emigrated from Canton province, China, to Canada in the early 1900s. She was born in China while her parents were on a business trip. The Chinese government declared her to be a Chinese citizen and blocked her departure to Canada until the age of three. Chinese culture was a positive component of her experiences as a child. In her own words:

"We lived in Duncan, B.C., a small Canadian city with a tiny Chinese community, but the concepts of Traditional Chinese Medicine were promoted on a daily basis. Children were urged to eat certain foods, or to take a certain herb to prevent or counter specific conditions or the weather which might bring on adverse conditions in the body. We were taught that certain foods would keep the skin clear, the eyes bright, and the bones strong.

"Dreams were believed to hold certain messages. Feng shui (wind/water as known by the Chinese, or geomancy as known by the British) and astrological relationships governed many decisions, including the careful selection of an appropriate name. It was extremely important that daily living habits and special occasions be planned to coincide with appropriate days or times of the year.

"The respect, reverence and homage paid to elders and ancestors and nature were an essential part of our physical, emotional, and spiritual well-being. Reincarnation was treated in a matter-of-fact manner along with the continual evolution of nature and life, the microcosm/macrocosm relationship of existence .... all these were part of our philosophical upbringing. Daoism, Buddhism, and Christianity all were interwoven and intertwined in our spiritual learning. Confucianism was part of the discipline. People prepared themselves for death and when death did occur, friends not only

mourned the passing, they also celebrated and rejoiced in the person's contribution to this life and transition to the next.

"Like many other Chinese families, we used TCM on a day-to-day basis, unless crisis care or hospitalization were needed. I occasionally witnessed people being healed with Chinese medicine methods after Western medicine had given up and death was said to be inevitable. In one instance, a family friend was seriously ill with abdominal pains his Western doctors could not diagnose.

"My parent's friend, Mr. Wong, was admitted to the local hospital and given only three to six weeks to live even though no medical diagnosis could be made. My father, a businessman, obtained the physician's permission to use TCM with Mr. Wong. My father used moxibustion and herbs, and other people came to the hospital and treated Mr. Wong with Qigong. Mr. Wong made a full recovery and lived another fifteen years, which came as no surprise to the Chinese community.

"There is a humorous side to this story. Moxibustion involves the burning of the herb Artemisia Vulgaris (moxa) to apply deep heat to the energy system underlying the skin. The aroma of the burning moxa permeated the hospital. The maintenance department searched for an electrical short circuit for three days before the cause of the odor was identified.

"Another early exposure I had to TCM came in the form of Mrs. Jung, a good family friend who practiced Qigong and Taiji. Mrs. Jung came to our home frequently and I learned some of her skills. She looked much younger than her actual age, and her movements were very agile, her body firm.

"During the time I was growing up, society expected people from all cultural groups to conform in both thought and action to all that was Western. Anything else was looked upon as superstition and open to ridicule. This meant burying my culture in public and conforming to the ways of the general population on the outside.

"In the privacy of the home, parents demanded strict adherence to Chinese cultural mores. This created a perpetual source of conflict *in children growing up in the Chinese community at that time. I resolved this conflict by taking scientific training in nursing and education to become a Western trained health professional and educator.*

"Then a tragic event occurred which motivated me to re-explore the values of my heritage, Qigong, and TCM. My father had developed hypertension and also Bell's Palsy, a one-sided paralysis of the face considered in Western medicine to be of unknown cause. Bell's palsy is usually self limited and disappears spontaneously in about two to eight weeks. He elected to be treated by our family physician, who prescribed several drugs. My father never was informed of any potential side effects from the drugs, or life threatening reactions. He had a severe drug reaction and died.

"This tragic incident created a severe conflict within me. I had experienced the wonders of Qigong and TCM as a child, but had suppressed this part of my life to practice within the bounds of scientifically acceptable Western medicine. It was extremely difficult for me to accept such a traumatic incident.

"In my position as a nurse, I noticed many problems Western medicine was experiencing, and even creating. I began to search long and hard, learning all I could about the healing arts of my heritage. I considered the positives and negatives of both Western medicine and TCM. I decided to take the best of both approaches and blend them together to form a better system in terms of both cost and effectiveness.

"I began to study TCM and Qigong seriously, and had the opportunity to apprentice with several masters. While in Taiwan on a special cultural exchange program to learn Chinese classical dancing and painting, I expanded the opportunity to include a six month apprenticeship with a Traditional Chinese Medicine and Qigong master. In the first few days I found I had a natural gift, what many would refer to as 'healing hands,' being able to elicit healing responses in some of my teacher's patients almost immediately.

"Later, I studied under masters in Vancouver, British Columbia,

Hong Kong, the People's Republic of China, and various parts of the United States. Most of my Qigong masters and teachers were humble people, but were excellent healers in terms of the successful recoveries I witnessed in their patients.

"I took classes in different schools of Qigong including Frolic of the Five Animals, White Crane, Taoist Qigong, Taiji, Shaolin, Microcosmic Orbit, and other lesser known styles. I once studied with the Venerable Grand Master of Wai Tan Kung in Taiwan. Eventually I developed my own healing system which has a Qigong style anyone can do and is adapted to people in the West who generally expect faster results. However, the system maintains the classic integrity of traditional Qigong."

As her Qigong skills became stronger with practice and experience, Dr. Chow confirmed what she had learned from the masters. *Almost any patient with any disease condition can be helped to some degree with Qigong.* She has a very high regard for Western medicine, but strongly believes that if the impersonal high technology of modern Western medicine were combined with ancient Eastern concepts and practices, mankind would be better served. She has devoted her life to the goals of fostering this unity and integration of Eastern and Western health and life systems for the ultimate benefit of all mankind.

Chapter 4: IN QUEST OF QI

"Traditional Chinese Medicine has been used in China for more than 5,000 years. It has been proven to be effective, can cure many diseases, and is economical."

Premier Zhou En-lai

"Gold is precious, but true qi is priceless."

Ancient Chinese Proverb

In March of 1990, Drs. Chow, Sancier and McGee were invited to visit China for an update on Qigong activities. Dr. Stephen Kong, my host on several trips to China, planned our trip. Dr. Kong has a Ph.D. in biomedical engineering and is currently President and Chairman of Sino-American Medical Technology Communications, International. He is very knowledgeable both in Western medicine and TCM and through his many connections was able to arrange Qigong-related meetings for us throughout China. We had the opportunity to learn about high quality Qigong research and treatment in a way many others would envy. Our first Qigong stop was at the Guangdong Provincial Traditional Chinese Medical College in Guangzhou (Canton).

At this point I would like to describe the medical system in China because it is so different from ours in the West. Two parallel systems of medical schools and hospitals exist in China. Traditional Chinese Medical schools grant degrees in TCM. TCM and Qigong are part of a philosophical system that pervades all aspects of daily living, maintains health, and prevents illness. They are based on underlying concepts such as the positive and negative, Yin and Yang, and the Five Elements Theory. The theories of TCM are touched upon in Chapter 5.

Graduates of TCM schools become employees of TCM

hospitals after completion of their academic studies. Many treatment modalities are used in TCM including Qigong, philosophy, meditation, Taiji (Tai Chi), martial arts, touch healing, physical therapy, special traditional Chinese massage therapies called Tuinah, Ahnmoh, nutritional concepts, herbs, moxibustion, cupping, dream therapy, Feng Shui, and acupuncture. All are based on energy concepts.

Western medical schools in China grant the equivalent of the M.D. degree, and their graduates become employees of a system of Western hospitals in China. These facilities employ the same methods commonly used in hospitals in North America and Europe, principally drugs and surgery. Until very recently, all physicians in both systems in China were salaried employees in government hospitals, and were paid poorly by standards in the West, about $50.00 U.S. per month. More recently, physicians have begun to open private offices where they see fee-for-service patients in the evening hours.

The government supports both Western and TCM systems financially, and one is not favored over the other. The cost of medical care for working people is shouldered by their employers. Medical care for the unemployed is paid by the Chinese government.

All TCM hospitals have a few Western trained physicians available on staff to provide treatment with Western methods, when that course of action seems most appropriate (such as surgery for thyroid tumors). All Western hospitals in China have been required by government regulations to have a department of TCM since 1957. Dr. Kong told us this occurred because TCM methods were popular among the people. In addition, Premier Zhou En-lai had declared, "Traditional Chinese Medicine has been used in China for more than 5,000 years. It has been proven to be effective, can cure many diseases, and is economical."

For several reasons a feeling of competition between the dual systems does not exist. Medical students in each program cross-train to some extent and learn the strong points of the parallel system.

Therefore, physicians in each system develop a respect for each other. There is no monetary reason to compete because physicians are salaried and their wages are low. Another is the absence of large corporations that promote treatments from which they profit, such as drug companies.

This cross-training produces benefits in research activities. Doctors of TCM who do research are able to receive assistance from Western trained physicians in evaluating their results, frequently using the modern high tech diagnostic equipment available only in Western hospitals. This level of cooperation is rare to absent in the West at this time. It could serve very well as a model for the health care system in the West.

When they become ill, people have free choice as to how they want to be treated. Those with acute medical problems, such as infections, burns, injuries, diabetes, and heart attacks, generally choose to go to a Western hospital for treatment. People with chronic conditions, such as arthritis, high blood pressure, headaches, bowel disorders, and allergies, usually choose to go to a TCM hospital. This system seems to work well except for a lack of modern facilities, equipment, and over-crowding.

CANTON (GUANGZHOU)

Now back to Canton. Our first stop was at the apartment of the retired dean of the TCM College who told us about the background of the school. After lunch we toured the Qigong department of the medical school hospital. Instructors in the Qigong department gave us a demonstration of methods taught in the school. Several masters emitted their qi at us to see how sensitive we were. Dr. Chow was quickly able to sense their qi, but Dr. Sancier and I were not as sensitive.

One of the Qigong masters interested me because he exemplified how seriously Qigong is taken in China. He had received his M.D. degree from a Chinese medical school in the Western system. He then took specialty training in surgery and worked in that field for many years. During that time he observed the effectiveness of Qigong treatment and began to study and practice Qigong himself.

Eventually, the surgeon became a Qigong master and gave up his practice of surgery to teach Qigong at the TCM school. I thought to myself that he must have witnessed some amazing results from Qigong for him to decide to make such an unusual career change.

Our visit was purposely short. That evening we flew on to Shanghai.

SHANGHAI

Our first visit in Shanghai was at the Shanghai Institute of TCM. Our hosts asked a Qigong master in their employ to join us to demonstrate a Qigong exercise he had developed which mimics the movements of a snake (in a vertical position). The master put his body through slithering motions. Everyone in the room wished he or she could be as limber as this Qigong master. By this time we had seen many variations of Qigong exercises, but this was the most unusual so far.

After tea our hosts took us to a room in which five patients were receiving individual treatments from five Qigong masters. It was like no other treatment room I have seen. The patients were lying either prone or supine on examination tables as they received treatments with emitted qi. Each Qigong master was holding a motionless hand over his patient's body at a distance of about two feet. Very seldom did a master ever touch a patient.

One of the patients was an old woman who lived with continuous pain from arthritis. At the end of her treatment she got up from the table and walked out of the room showing no signs of discomfort or difficulty. In a few moments she returned to retrieve the cane she had been using for many years, her face red with embarrassment. She felt so good after the treatment she had forgotten the cane and left it behind.

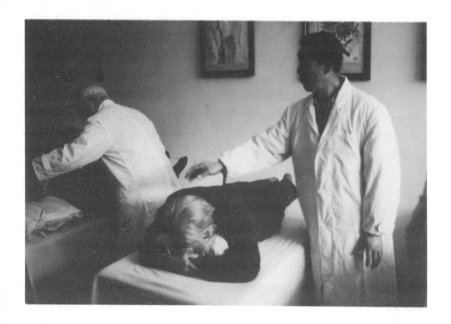

Figure 1. Qigong masters emitting qi to patients in a Shanghai clinic.

Later that day we visited George Shen, M.D., Director of Research at the Shanghai Qigong Research Institute, affiliated with the Shanghai College of Traditional Chinese Medicine. Dr. Shen had conducted a series of scientific studies on the measurable energies which Qigong masters emit from their hands when they treat patients. This energy flows from the "laogong energy point" in the palm (also called Pericardium 8).

Various forms of energies have been detected. These include Raman spectra, ultraviolet spectra, infrasonic emission at low frequencies in the one to twelve hertz (cycles per second) range, microwave emissions, magnetic field generation, and electrostatic field generation.

The amounts of energy emitted are generally from 100 to 1,000 times what can be measured coming from the laogong points of ordinary individuals. The energies diminish with the square of the distance, and can be blocked by a thin lead shield. Thus they appear to behave according to physical laws, but there is no scientific explanation why the levels from Qigong masters are so high.

Dr. Shen showed us photographic slides taken during one of his studies. He measured microwave activity from the laogong point in the palm of a Qigong master both in a resting state and the special Qigong treatment state. The level of microwave activity increased dramatically in the latter.

Dr. Kong, our host, told us of a hospital in the countryside near Shanghai that specializes in the treatment of people with Parkinson's disease, but our tight schedule prevented us from visiting the facility. People with Parkinson's disease are admitted as in-patients for two months and receive treatment exclusively with Qigong. About eighty percent of patients are said to improve. This contrasts sharply with the usual down-hill course seen in people with this normally discouraging disease.

BEIJING

After spending a productive three days in Shanghai we flew on to Beijing. Dr. Kong lives in Beijing, so he scheduled most of our activities there.

Guo Lin Qigong

The first morning in Beijing, we went to a park next to a canal. It was a clear day with a cold, brisk north wind, the temperature in the low twenties (F.). The weather was no deterrent for about seventy cancer victims who had come to the park to learn a style of Qigong known as Guo Lin Qigong.

This style of Qigong was created by a woman named Guo Lin in the late 1960s. Guo Lin had cancer of the uterus which was treated with surgery, but the cancer returned in her bladder. During a second operation surgeons removed part of her bladder, but this also failed to cure her. When the cancer returned again, her doctors told her she was untreatable and would be dead in six months.

Guo Lin was familiar with Qigong because her grandfather had taught her as a child. Instead of practicing exercises developed by others, she decided to innovate. She was aware that with serious practice, people often develop the ability to feel their own body energies and balances. She followed her own sensations and created a style of Qigong that *felt right* for her.

She practiced her new form of Qigong diligently. Gradually the cancer shrank, then disappeared completely. She lived cancer-free many more years and died of other causes in 1984.

Guo Lin Qigong is a walking form of Qigong that looks unique. In the main version, the feet meet the ground very deliberately heel first and the hands pass back and forth in a horizontal plane just below the navel. Vocal sounds are timed with these movements that sound like "Chee-chee-hoo, Chee-chee-hoo." According to theories of TCM, certain sounds may affect specific organ systems in the body.

We observed groups of people walking around in the park in a single file saying in unison, "Chee-chee-hoo, Chee-chee-hoo." The smoothness of their movements was impressive. Other people clustered in small groups to receive instruction in variations of Guo Lin Qigong. Only people who have used the method to effect a personal cure from advanced cancer are allowed to become instructors in the method.

Dr. Kong had arranged for us to meet Guo Lin's husband, Mr. Lin Xiao, an outspoken proponent of his wife's work. We also met several survivors of advanced cancer. One man told us his liver cancer disappeared completely after he practiced Guo Lin Qigong. Another described how he was victorious in his battle against cancer of the pancreas. These two cures are significant because patients with cancers of the liver and pancreas generally have survival rates that approach zero.

At the end of our visit to the park, a woman of about fifty approached us and, in fluent English, offered to give us a personal demonstration of the method. She was a Western trained medical doctor who had been battling cancer for several years. Our small party went to a nearby hotel and warmed up with some tea. This physician then showed us variations of Guo Lin Qigong, including all of its intricate and graceful movements.

Figure 2. Guo Lin leading cancer patients in her style of Qigong. Photo courtesy of the Guo Lin Research Society.

We were told that over one million cancer patients in China now practice Guo Lin Qigong on a daily basis. Guo Lin's work is carried on through the *Guo Lin Research Society.*

The Red Cross Hospital

Our next stop was at the Red Cross Hospital in Beijing, a facility which specializes in using Qigong to treat cancer. All patients were in this hospital by their own choice, having asked their doctors to refer them to a facility that concentrates on treating cancer with Qigong. Other methods of treatment also were used in the hospital, such as Western medicines and herbs.

Staff doctors asked two cancer patients to join us in the meeting room. One had advanced cancer of the liver, the other advanced cancer of the lung. After six months of treatment both were feeling good, eating normally, and had regained weight they had lost. They were not cancer free, but their doctors said their tumors were continuing to diminish in size. Both men verified to us that their overall state of health was improving.

X-Ray Vision

While we were in Beijing, Dr. Kong introduced us to several Qigong masters who purportedly could look directly into the body and describe what they saw, as if they had x-ray vision. Their descriptions could then be translated into medical terms and diagnoses. One evening we met Master Yuan Xiao-Jie, a man of about thirty, who had been asked to examine the three "honored guests" with his x-ray vision.

Master Yuan first told us a humorous story from his childhood. As a small boy, he discovered his x-ray vision abilities and found he could look into the bodies of women and tell when they had become pregnant. He thought this was something special so he went around his neighborhood spreading this interesting news. Many times he did so before a woman herself knew she was pregnant, and his actions caused much alarm and embarrassment, but he said he was always correct.

Master Yuan leaned back in his chair, squinted his eyes, and looked at Dr. Chow. Suddenly his eyes opened wide in surprise and he said, "Oh! You are a Qigong master!" Qigong masters have large balanced energy patterns around their bodies that are easily seen by people who are sensitive to subtle energies.

He looked at Dr. Sancier and said, "You're ordinary." Dr. Sancier was crestfallen by this pronouncement. He had been practicing Qigong exercises for some time and I believe he expected more recognition for his efforts.

Master Yuan glanced at me quickly and said I, too, was ordinary. Then he looked at me again, squinted his eyes, and gave me some bad news. He said the left main artery of my heart showed fatty deposits, but the process was early. I wasn't very happy to hear this because my father died of a heart attack.

Most Qigong masters who have this unusual x-ray vision ability have had no formal medical training. They describe organs they see according to location, color, or size, but are unfamiliar with medical terms or diagnoses. Usually their descriptions must be translated into medical terms by others.

Dr. Kong told us of a female TCM doctor with this ability who was asked to participate in a study. All patients first had their problems diagnosed with conventional Western methods and all had conditions that were obvious on x-rays or imaging tests. The TCM doctor then used her x-ray vision to look into their bodies and commit herself to a Western diagnosis. Her diagnoses corresponded with the established diagnoses ninety-five percent of the time.

More Qigong Masters

Because of our tight travel schedule, Dr. Kong brought five Qigong masters from Harbin (Manchuria) to visit with us in Beijing.

All five stayed in our hotel, so we shared many meals and many hours with them. Three of these masters were either doctors of TCM, or "Qigong doctors." The term "Qigong doctor" is applied to a person who is trained to treat people with Qigong, but has not gone through the years of training required to be a doctor of TCM.

Two of these individuals had developed unique electronic instruments. The instruments were described to us because they were large and not easily transported from Harbin to Beijing. One instrument was said to measure energies emitted by Qigong masters. We were told that about 100 Qigong masters had been tested on the instrument so far, and most of them emitted different mixtures of measurable energy. To complicate matters further, some Qigong masters with proven healing records didn't emit any energies the machine could detect.

China has a great need for such an instrument. Dr. Kong told us that some dishonest people have claimed to be Qigong masters and charged for worthless treatments. The government is trying to find a way to test and certify Qigong masters, so impostors can be weeded out.

I was more interested in the second instrument, which was the product of thirty years of research in the family of Dr. Zhao Zuo An, a doctor of TCM. I was examined with this instrument later in the year when I visited Dr. Zhao's office in Harbin.

The masters from Harbin were an interesting mixture of people. Dr. Ma Qui Yang published Qigong magazines that are distributed throughout China. He told us about Qigong related activities and research in institutes, hospitals, and medical schools throughout China. Two other masters from Harbin were women who participated in demonstrations of qi.

In a demonstration of the power of emitted qi, the Harbin masters asked Dr. Chow to stand in the middle of the room and close her eyes. Dr. Ma Qui Yang stood behind her, and the two women masters positioned themselves in front of her. The three masters worked in unison to try to exert an energy field that would move Dr.

Chow either forward or backward. Without much difficulty, they moved her several feet across the room.

When my turn came, the masters found I was much more difficult to move. Finally, in a super effort on the part of all three of them, I was pushed forward. If I had not taken a step forward I would have fallen on my face. The sensation was as if someone had placed a board across my upper back, then pushed on it.

Dr. Sancier was moved more easily. The masters had no problem making him walk forward and backward six to eight feet at a time, the distance being constrained only by the size of the room.

Later, after returning home, I examined video tapes of this experience. I was able to confirm that we did move in unison with the direction of the Qigong masters' arm movements, so it appeared to be a valid experience.

In the second demonstration of qi, one of the female Qigong masters from Harbin displayed an unusual talent. She produced a piece of glass from her pocket and handed it to us for inspection. The section of glass was about three inches long by one inch wide, and about as thick as a window pane.

When we handed the glass back to her she placed it in her mouth and, with a loud crunch, bit about one inch off the end of it, then proceeded to methodically chew it up. As she chewed, her jaws worked deliberately, making a loud crunching sound that could be heard throughout the room. After about three or four minutes, she swallowed and it was gone.

She opened her mouth and showed there was no sign of any cut, bleeding, or residual glass. The amazing thing about this demonstration was that she had extensive dental work, including bridges, that did not appear to have been damaged. Eating glass certainly has no practical value, but it does demonstrate once again that people have a higher potential than we suspect. Many people have such weak digestive qi they have difficulty swallowing and digesting any food, let alone glass.

The "National Institutes of Health" of Chinese Medicine

One day Dr. Kong took us to visit China's leading research institute in TCM. He said that the organization had as much prestige in China as the National Institutes of Health in the United States. The work of the Institute is carried out in a building about ten stories tall in downtown Beijing.

Dr. Shen Shao-gong, Director of the Institute, took us on a tour of the facilities. As we walked from floor to floor, he introduced us to researchers who described experiments they were performing. Most people outside of China are unaware of the quantity and quality of research that has been done in TCM since about 1980.

The Chinese have used double-blind studies in researching the effectiveness of herbs. Ancient concepts of energy pathways and energy points have been confirmed in both China and France by tracking the course of radio-isotopes. They have verified energy channels and points shown on ancient charts and bronze dolls. We asked how the ancients might have discovered this system. The best explanation appears to be that some of them were able to see these energy points and pathways, much as sensitive people can seen auras of energy around the body today, and others have "x-ray" vision.

We were shown an instrument which can automatically measure the twelve pulses that doctors of TCM take on the radial arteries at the wrist when they are trying to establish an energy diagnosis. "Pulse diagnosis" is one of the diagnostic methods in TCM, along with inspecting the tongue and taking a verbal medical history. We were asked not to photograph the instrument because of the risk of scientific espionage. The entire tour was an eye-opening experience.

Dr. Chow Passes the Test

We had spent nearly one week in Beijing visiting with the masters from Harbin. Near the end of our stay, Dr. Ma announced that he wanted to verify Dr. Chow's claim of being a Qigong master, declaring that he wanted to "feel Dr. Chow's qi." Apparently he was skeptical that powerful Qigong masters could exist outside China.

We had little time for sleeping on this trip and were forced to be indoors a majority of the time because of cold weather. Another negative health factor for us was that most men in China smoke excessively, so we had been breathing heavily polluted air for two weeks. Dr. Chow, normally the picture of optimal health, was developing a head cold. Conditions were not perfect for the test but she rose to the challenge.

She stood about twenty-five feet from Dr. Ma, assumed a very straight posture, and breathed deeply to build up her qi. She emitted qi at Dr. Ma from a spot between her eye brows (the "third eye") as well as from her total body. Ma's eyes enlarged in surprise as he felt her qi and said, "Yes, you are indeed a powerful Qigong master."

Afterward, Dr. Ma reported that he at first had a generalized sense of a strong qi, then it was suddenly a concentrated powerful force directed at his chest and "third eye."

This concluded our joint trip and the three of us prepared to return home. We had been immersed in Qigong-related activities about eighteen hours a day for two weeks. Instead of being tired, we felt energized by the experience. We had seen many things we would never forget and had been in the presence of powerful Qigong masters most of the time.

HARBIN

Later in the year I visited China again and flew to Harbin, near the Russian border in northeastern China. One purpose for the trip was to visit the private clinic of Dr. Zhao Zuo An.

Dr. Zhao was a man of about fifty who had come from a long line of doctors of TCM. He was away on an emergency when we came to the clinic, so we met his son, also a doctor of TCM. Dr. Kong and I went to Zhao's clinic to see the diagnostic instrument described to us earlier in the year in Beijing. Zhao's family had been developing the device for over thirty years, and this was the only prototype. Zhao's son ushered us directly into a treatment room. He was friendly but busy, and didn't waste any time with the usual Chinese greeting rituals of tea and small talk.

The instrument consisted of six electronic boxes connected to an oscilloscope with an untidy collection of wires. Young Zhao offered to show us how the machine functioned by performing a screening test on me.

I was asked to lay down on the examination table and take off my shirt. Zhao attached two metal bands over saline-soaked sponges on my wrists. He explained that the wetness was needed to assure a good electrical contact. The wrist bands were attached to the menagerie of little boxes with wires.

He then took a probe that was connected to the machine with a wire, and pressed its cold blunt end on my skin about one inch lateral to the edge of my breast bone (sternum). He tested energy points up one side of my chest and down the other. During the examination, he explained to us that these points represent different organs and functions in the energy system of the body, very much like the keys on a computer keyboard.

Zhao moved from point to point on my chest rapidly, then switched his attention to test points on my scalp. Starting from behind one ear he checked a string of points across the top of my head, finishing at a point behind the opposite ear.

As each point was tested, Dr. Kong and I watched a wave pattern form on the oscilloscope. Zhao was so skilled in the method, he needed only a quick glance at the oscilloscope before moving on to the next point. The entire evaluation was completed in less than two minutes. Zhao paused, then told me his unpleasant finding. He said the test showed I had early disease in the left main artery of my heart. This was the same impression reached by three masters with x-ray vision who had examined me in Beijing.

Zhao placed the probe over my heart point showing us how the shape of the wave on the oscilloscope differed from normal. He asked if I had experienced any discomfort when he tested the heart point. I told him I had felt a mildly painful electrical stinging that was not present when the other points were tested. Zhao said that patients generally feel discomfort when positive points are tested.

Dr. Kong said that the machine had undergone a thorough evaluation in cooperation with Western trained physicians. During its development, tests were performed on volunteers who had received physical examinations and were found to be in good health. One of these people was employed as a secretary at a nearby hospital.

On her first evaluation, everyone involved was shocked when the readings indicated the presence of a cancer of the stomach. The Zhaos referred the woman to a gastroenterologist who performed a gastroscopy (a visual examination of the inside of the stomach with a scope). At that time no abnormality was found.

Every two months the woman was examined with Zhao's instrument and by the gastroenterologist with his gastroscope. The oscilloscope readings on Zhao's machine continually read positive; the direct visual exams continued to be normal. However, eighteen months later, a small abnormality was found with the gastroscope and a biopsy was taken. The biopsy confirmed the presence of a very early cancer of the stomach. Apparently the cancer was present as some kind of electromagnetic disturbance for at least eighteen months before it could be found by the most accurate conventional diagnostic test available.

Zhao told us the instrument had been evaluated in patients whose diagnoses previously were established with Western medical techniques and his method agreed with the known diagnoses ninety-five percent of the time. Therefore, the device appears to have great potential in the early screening of patients who are entering the medical system for diagnostic evaluations. By narrowing a problem down early in an evaluation, many costly, risky, and unnecessary tests can be avoided. This could save time, discomfort, and substantial sums of money.

Zhao's instrument has an additional application. After a treatment is begun, a patient can be tested again immediately, even minutes later. If a treatment is going to be helpful, the oscilloscope readings will change slightly in the direction of normal. If the treatment is not going to help, the patterns on the oscilloscope will not change. This application allows physicians to change their approaches quickly to those that will be more effective.

This instrument has great promise, but remains undeveloped at this time because of a lack of funds. Dr. Kong says the machine needs to be miniaturized and provided with a means of printing out a written interpretation. Technically this would be fairly simple.

QINHUANGDAO

Dr. Kong and I took an overnight train from Harbin to Qinhuangdao, located on the Pacific Ocean about five hours east of Beijing by train. Qinhuangdao and nearby Beidehe are in a resort area of China. Hundreds of thousands of Chinese people enjoy the sandy beaches of the area during the warm months. It is a delightful area, uncrowded, unpolluted, and called the "summer capital" because so many of the top leaders of China move to Beidehe during that season.

We came to Qinhuangdao to see a powerful Qigong master whom Dr. Kong had recently met and befriended. In June of 1990 Dr. Kong had visited my home in the United States and showed me a video tape of Master Lu Lau Shu in action.

On the tape we saw the master outdoors in a courtyard with several of his patients. They all were standing facing the sun with their eyes closed, and the sun could be seen as a small bright circle with sharply defined borders. Master Lu and his patients opened their eyes and stared directly at the sun for several minutes. Master Lu explained that they were absorbing energy from the sun.

Something very strange happened. We saw the diameter of the sun gradually enlarge ten to fifteen times its normal size, its light intensity dim, and its normally sharp margins become poorly defined.

It looked as though a large filter had been placed over the sun, which caused its light to dim and disperse. Something else happened that was highly unusual. A triangularly shaped band of green light came straight down from the sun and surrounded Master Lu.

Another segment of the tape showed Master Lu lecturing to a group of about forty people. As he talked, he emitted healing energy. Many people appeared to react by moving back and forth while others uttered a variety of vocal tones. One woman began to thrash around by bending at the waist and cranking her upper body around in circles, up and down. Two people were engaged in a loud conversation, almost shouting into each other's faces. Kong said they were speaking Chinese words, but not saying anything that could be understood. About two-thirds of the people present were eventually involved in some form of unusual activity. Master Lu says that these actions represent the release of energy blockages, are beneficial, and can take many forms.

The tape showed Master Lu and his helpers emitting their qi at several people who had serious diseases. One woman with a brain cancer had radiation burns on the back of her head from her x-ray treatment. After only one Qigong treatment, her headaches went away and her next scanning test showed the cancer was smaller.

Another patient was an eighty-one year old man with cancer of the lung. His x-ray before Qigong treatment showed a mass in the lower right chest, immediately to the right of his heart. Master Lu treated the elderly man with emitted qi for thirty minutes daily, for twenty-one days in succession. X-rays were taken immediately before the treatment began, and the day after the treatments were stopped. During this short period of three weeks the cancer disappeared. Cancer cells were present in sputum smears (produced by coughing) before the treatments, but were absent in four consecutive sputum smears after the treatments.

These x-rays were available to us on videotape. Dr. Kong asked the hospital's administrator if we could see the originals, but the request was denied. Several Western trained doctors were envious of what a Qigong master was achieving outside of their own medical system, and did not want to help him in any way.

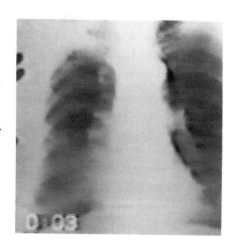

Figure 3. X-ray of an eighty-one year old man with lung cancer, before Qigong treatment. The cancer forms a shadow next to his heart (left side of heart in photo).

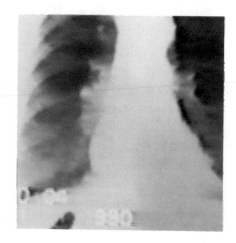

Figure 4. Twenty-two days later, a radiologist read this film (among others) as showing the cancer had disappeared. The shadow next to the heart is gone, and the heart border is sharp.

When we met Master Lu, I was impressed by his vitality and enthusiasm. He was forty at the time and the picture of good health. We asked him about the background of Fan Teng Qigong.

Master Lu said the method was 2,500 years old and had been kept secret in a local Buddhist order until 1987. For all of that time, special secrets of the method had been passed on from one master to a chosen disciple, and now had been passed on to him. The old master of the method was still living, but Master Lu steadfastly refused to reveal his identity. He said his elderly master had informed him it was time to share Fan Teng Qigong with the world.

I asked Master Lu what would happen to the secrets of the method if he were killed on the way home. He told us that was not going to happen because he knew when he was going to die. He knew he had plenty of time before he would need to pass on the secrets of the method to a chosen successor. He might be right because the chain of succession has not been broken in 2,500 years.

When wine was served with lunch Master Lu noticed I was not drinking mine and asked why. I explained that I seldom drank alcohol because I like to keep a clear head. Master Lu said he could fix this problem very easily. He placed his hand over my glass for about twenty seconds, then announced that all of the alcohol had been dissipated. When I tasted the wine the alcohol bite was gone and when I drank it I felt none of the usual effects of alcohol.

Dr. Kong said that scientific tests had been performed to see if Qigong masters could alter the alcohol content of wine and that the experiments documented that they could. Dr. Kong added that the chemical patterns of flower aromas also had been altered by Qigong masters, as shown with sensitive detection instruments.

After lunch Master Lu wanted to demonstrate some effects of qi on me, a common practice among masters in China. He rolled up a newspaper and asked me to hold one end against my palm, then placed his hand over the other end (about eighteen inches from mine). Within seconds I had to jerk my hand away to keep from being burned from a sudden burst of intense heat, most likely the result of emitted infra-red energy scientists have verified.

Master Lu then asked me to stand with my eyes closed while he walked about fifty feet away. He emitted his qi at me and pushed me backwards and forwards so violently that I had to be fast on my feet to keep from falling down. Master Lu's energy was much more powerful than that of the masters from Harbin who had a difficult time moving me at all.

Master Lu asked us to go outside into a patio on this clear, crisp September day. It was one o'clock in the afternoon and the sun was shining brightly. Master Lu held his hand over my abdomen for about one minute while Dr. Kong translated that Lu was transferring energy to my "dantian" (an energy storage area in the abdomen just below the navel). I was told that I could now look at the sun without injury to my eyes!

I had heard of this phenomenon, and had seen it on video tape. I also was aware of the dangers usually associated with looking at the sun. An old Ripley's *Believe It Or Not* column came to mind about a man in India who stared at the sun and went blind. It doesn't take much exposure to burn out your eyes.

Very warily I looked at the sun, then quickly looked away. Gradually I looked at the sun for longer and longer periods. After a timid build up period, I stared directly at the sun for about forty-five seconds. I was confident at this point that I could continue to look at the sun without injury, if I chose to do so. This was long enough to convince me that this was really happening.

When I finally looked away, there were no bright spots, no pain, watering, or damage to my eyes. Fifteen minutes later my eyes returned to their normal level of hyper-sensitivity and I had to use my dark glasses again.

When I returned home I related this experience to Dr. Chow. She was very happy and excited about my experience, but was not surprised. Being able to stare at the sun is quite common for Qigong masters and she frequently has done this.

Chapter 5: PHILOSOPHY AND CONCEPTS

"Each person carries his own doctor inside him. They come to us not knowing that truth. We are at our best when we give the doctor who resides within each patient a chance to go to work."
Albert Schweitzer

"Giving individuals the power to determine and manage their own health and destinies is the secret of true healing."
Effie Poy Yew Chow

The Chow Integrated Healing System (The Chow System) is a pragmatic system that combines modern Western health practices, ancient Traditional Chinese Medicine, and Dr. Chow's original concepts of a total integrated approach to health of the body, mind, and spirit. Qigong is the basic underlying component of The Chow System. It is based on the classic Chinese theory that a powerful energy system exists in the body, and that energy (qi) flows through known energy pathways. The pathways are referred to as channels, or meridians. The qi system is as distinct as the respiratory and nervous systems. If qi patterns are disrupted by emotional distress, environmental exposures, or any number of factors, a person becomes susceptible to disease. When this disruption of energy is rebalanced, health is restored.

In this integrated approach, a person's body, mind, and spirit are one, interacting with people, the immediate environment, and the Universe. Clients play a central role in their therapy. Fitness and preventive health are emphasized and stress and tension often are seen as common precursors to disease. Another concept is that all true healing originates from a higher power, and that effective healing occurs only when a healer or practitioner has facilitated the flow of qi from this higher source.

In this and the following two chapters, Dr. Chow touches on her philosophy of healing, and outlines her approaches which often lead to the miraculous responses presented. Please bear in mind that this system is quite complex, and only the basic concepts are presented in this book.

CONCEPTS OF THE CHOW INTEGRATED HEALING SYSTEM

The Chow Integrated Healing System is comprised of many important components, theories, and principles. As a summary, ten of the most important basic concepts for initial practice are:

1) Get at least eight hugs a day, and be "in touch"
2) Get at least three Belly-Aching-Laughs-A-Day
3) Maintain a positive mental attitude
4) Maintain proper posture and breathe with the diaphragm (not the chest)
5) Meditate daily
6) Good nutrition, supplements, and perhaps herbs
7) Practice the right type of exercise - Qigong exercises
8) Be at peace with yourself and others
9) Live the qi energy concept
10) Give and receive lots of love

Love is the most important ingredient underlying the Chow Integrated Healing System. Without love, all the highest aspirations and goodwill are empty dreams or actions. Without love, life qi is empty. And of course, without qi, life is naught. Let me share with you this poem on love by Emmett Fox which relates to my system of healing.

LOVE

There is no difficulty that enough love will not conquer;
No disease that enough love will not heal;
No door that enough love will not open;
No gulf that enough love will not bridge;
No wall that enough love will not throw down;
No sin that enough love will not redeem...

It makes no difference how deeply seated may be the trouble;
How hopeless the outlook;
How muddled the tangle;
How great the mistake;
A sufficient realization of love will dissolve it all...

If only you could love enough, you would be the happiest and
most powerful being in this world.

A good Qigong master or "healer" must be free from the self-ego. The altruistic ego is all right. Healing qi is ever-existing in the natural Universe. A healer is a clear catalyst who can facilitate the rebalancing of qi in nature and in the individual to enable self healing.

A healer must know when to call upon other resources. Some practitioners may see a patient weekly for a long time with no significant results. If I don't see any changes within six months (sometimes even three months, depending upon the condition), I am already considering alternative resources for the person. Happily this is needed infrequently.

Personal Evaluation

The following pages describe how I interact with people who come to see me for a private consultation, or for training. However, all of these concepts and approaches apply to anyone who wants to use Qigong to enhance his or her health and healing.

People who come to me are referred to as "clients" instead of "patients" because the terms imply different things. A patient is someone who goes to a practitioner and expects something to be done to them. In contrast, a client has the right to knowledge, has the power of making decisions, and is a partner in the healing process. From the very first contact, clients are helped to understand it is essential for them to participate in the healing process. This responsibility increases as they learn more skills.

The healing process is a mutual educational experience rather than the usual patient-practitioner relationship. For example, working with people who have serious illnesses, especially AIDS, paralysis, and cancer, teaches us the ultimate in loyalty, compassion, and love. It is a privilege for me to be part of a client's healing process.

When clients schedule appointments, they are asked to prepare a self-written chronology of their condition(s), and bring records of a recent evaluation by a physician. The chronology includes their progress, services or treatments they have sought, what has or has not helped, what kinds of medications they have used and are using, what they presently are capable of doing, and how they are restricted.

Writing the chronology forces them to sit down and think through their condition and its evolution, and about life events. Frequently they gain a new insight to a problem. Often comments like this are made, "A very revealing and wonderful understanding or enlightenment came through as I was writing my chronology--many things that I had never thought about." When this happens, the healing process already has begun.

Clients are requested to keep a written daily journal during therapy and note all of the positive things that take place. If there is an issue they need to discuss, they are asked to write it down as a positive goal they would like to reach, rather than simply stating the problem. The journal is essential because writing reinforces, or "seals in," the healing energy.

Writing is the only thing we do that requires such complete

concentration. Other things can be done in combination with something else. For example, we can listen to the radio and wash dishes, read and carry on a conversation. However, when a person is writing, it is most difficult to listen to or follow anything else that may be occurring.

When clients arrive at the office they fill out a questionnaire. Photographs may be taken before and after therapy. Often videotapes are made to "capture the moment," and become a wonderful educational tool for clients to review their progress. Clients are asked to see a physician for an updated evaluation of their condition before therapy, especially if they haven't been to one during the past year. If they don't have a physician, several are recommended. This helps to build a bridge between Qigong and the Western medical system, and is also a means of cross-education with physicians.

After therapy, clients are encouraged to see their physicians again so progress can be documented. When a significant "miraculous" improvement occurs, particularly in a short time, they are asked to see the same physician right away. This frequently proves to be an eye-opening revelation and education for the physician.

The usual TCM diagnostic steps are taken, including a medical-social history, blood pressure, and vital signs. Body, mind, spirit, and environmental concepts are discussed. Emotional or spiritual problems may be the underlying cause of a physical problem, and the converse is also true. Major and often even minor events in people's lives have great significance: even events five years prior to the beginning of the current situation, or even in childhood, may be related causally.

Individuals have a chance to explore past events or relationships. However, time constraints necessitate that clients plan for today and the future, and not spend excessive time delving into past problems. Many people have no dreams or plans for the future, or a reason for wanting to get well. In such cases, focusing on the past generally is not helpful nor an efficacious use of time.

Clients who have serious conditions are asked if they really want to get well, and this may seem like a very silly question. They often are surprised and say, "Of course I want to get well." Frequently they may say that, but their actions may indicate otherwise. All too frequently when therapies are recommended they do not make the effort to comply. The next question is, "If you really want to get well, for what reason do you want to get well?" People must have a purpose for getting well, often some thing or reason beyond concerns about their health. For example, they may want to get better so they will be healthy in time for their only daughter's wedding. Perhaps they want to visit their mother country which they left in their youth and never saw again, or do anything else that is important to them. In complex cases, it is often not enough to just want to get better.

Clients are asked to redefine their goals, dreams, and even fantasies, and not be limited by a fear of appearing to be ridiculous, or by the apparent insignificance of what they are thinking. They are asked to write down everything, and the more they write the better.

Clients need to decide whether or not they are willing to work at becoming healthy and well. Some people shop for "healers" and miracle cures, yet are not willing to follow the advice they receive. Consequently, they never give the healing system a chance to work. Sometimes people must become aware that this is what they have been doing.

Continuing Therapy

In carrying out the above, therapy has already begun. Next, clients begin to learn proper breathing, posture, and meditation. These are covered in detail later. Usually they will begin to feel a little better after the first session; pain may diminish and their energy level may rise enough for them to notice a difference. Even in clients with serious problems such as a paralysis, miraculous progress has occurred in the first session such as being able to stand up and walk by themselves.

Next, they learn one or two Qigong exercises, such as the "Heavenly Stretch," and "Hip Rotation" exercises (described in Chapter 7). Different exercises may be selected according to what is indicated by the client's condition. Clients might learn how to apply acupressure on themselves. Usually acupuncture needles are not used in the first session. Clients need to sense that they are helping themselves, becoming responsible for their own therapy.

Everyone needs to realize that he or she is the greatest instrument ever created, and the greatest miracle on earth! The job of the healer is to help clients maximize their own instrument, not to depend on the instruments of others. For example, if clients use music to calm themselves, instead of listening to their own internal music and learning ways to calm themselves, they become dependent upon another "crutch," even though it may be a pleasant one. Before they can become well, they must discard all of their "crutches," including that new one, and the process is going to take longer. This system takes a much shorter time because they don't get hooked on new crutches that must later be abandoned.

Healing is a fascinating subject. Often clients need help in ways that people ordinarily would not associate with medical care. Many different kinds of problems in clients' lives can block the healing process. When clients are being stressed by financial problems, attempts are made to create a job or career opportunity. When they are stressed because they are lonely, introductions may be arranged with people with whom they may be compatible. These types of stresses must be resolved before a healing process can begin to work.

It is common for people to have many problems in their interpersonal relationships. Clients are asked to make a list of the positive things about themselves, people who are close to them, and what each person needs to work out. They are asked to write out exactly what they expect from their relationship with a family member, or with a "significant other." Many people have no idea what they really expect from others, or even from themselves.

Often, when clients become depressed, or find themselves

suffering from low self-esteem, they can't think of anything good about themselves. In these cases I ask them to pull out the "positive me" file they prepared and read it. More often than not, this action has helped to improve their mood.

Support System

People need a support system, whether it consists of families, selected friends, or associates. Even animals and plants can be called a support system because what one needs is a friendly surrounding. We need people and things to respond to positively, people who will give us joy and pleasure. If you do not have a family, you need to find friends in whom you can trust and confide, people you respect. Everyone, whether consciously aware of it or not, needs someone with whom they can talk openly.

A Time to Heal

When a healer becomes actively involved in a healing process, many factors should be taken into consideration. For example, when a person is fearful and resistant, it is not wise to attempt a healing. The healer must use skills to reduce any fear or resistance the client is experiencing.

It is not wise to work on clients after they have over-eaten, when they are too hungry or tired, or after they have exercised strenuously. When these conditions are present, an attempted healing may lead to reactions which are the opposite of normal responses.

The healer/client relationship is like an educational process. Role modeling is very important in many ways. A healer must be healthy, otherwise he or she may give the client what is referred to as "garbage energy." Sick people are quite vulnerable to picking up this garbage energy, and it can make them worse. Conversely, if the healer is not in good health, he or she can pick up the client's garbage energy. The healer must work to get back into a balanced state before attempting a healing and should possess the knowledge and skills needed for this.

Empowerment and Prioritizing Time for Yourself

A core cause of illness is the sense of loss-of-control and self-esteem, a feeling that we are at the mercy of our environment, or of other people. When we are well, we often find it impossible to take time for ourselves, or to do what we want. Illness forces us to turn inward, to take care of ourselves and to make time for ourselves. When ill, people find it easier to focus on their own problems and to receive attention from others. When we are well, most of us feel that we should always be doing things for others. This satisfies our own egos because doing things for others makes us feel good.

When we do take time for ourselves, we subconsciously feel extremely guilty, or that we don't deserve this luxury. This may indicate a lack of self-esteem. We must learn that it is all right to reserve time for ourselves, and it is preferable to learn this before an illness strikes. Some people even benefit from an illness: it can become a powerful tool for manipulating others, even though they may not be consciously aware of doing so.

Once people become ill, self-esteem drops even further. In order to help them regain self-esteem as quickly as possible, I never do anything *to* a person right away without his or her participation. I always work *with* them: this is why clients begin learning about breath, posture, and meditation first as part of Qigong. Even when clients are being treated with emitted qi and they can feel some improvement, they must understand that they are a partner in this improvement, that we need to work together. Thus begins the step of empowerment for the client. As they develop and enhance their own internal qi, they will continue to gain more control over themselves, take control over their own lives, and to continue their healing process. That is one of the most important things they must learn. It is a phenomenal experience to watch people feel a sense of "power" as they discover that they have been responsible for their own improvement. (The word power is being used here in a positive way.)

Nothing Really Is New

Many of these concepts came directly out of my own deliberations and experiences, not necessarily from other sources. However, there really is nothing new in this Universe. Old concepts become modernized, recycled, and integrated into current time and place. Whenever possible, we redesign old concepts so they can be more effective now than they were in the past. Knowledge is recycled all of the time. Whether we know it or not, we innately pick up knowledge that has existed previously. Clients learn that everything there is to know is already within themselves.

A healer must be a facilitator who can bring this inner knowledge to the surface, and activate the built-in healer that is present within all of us. A good healer is an effective catalyst, or conductor, for the movement of the ever-present healing qi from the Universe to the client. A healer's responsibility is to teach people how to use this healing qi.

After treating many thousands of clients, I still marvel at and become excited with the miracles that occur daily in my work. I encourage people to maintain a sense of reverence and wonder at the magnificence, magic, and miracle of life. We should keep the child that lives within us alive and appreciate these wonders of life, these gifts. That, in itself, is what healing is all about and what gives us life. We should live each day to the fullest, instead of just existing. "Plan as if to live forever; live as if to die tomorrow."

You may have heard or read all of this before, but not in the same context. I advise my clients and students: "Listen well, even though it is repeated a hundred times, for at the one-hundred-and-first time, you may hear something that might be extremely valuable for you, or might be *the* key to unlocking that greater wisdom which is within yourself." If people leave their minds open and really listen, they may hear something new each time something is repeated. Their lives have been evolving and changing, so each time is not the same. Also, when they hear what seems to be the same information, a little change in presentation, or combining it with another concept or action can make a world of difference. Nothing is constant; the only constant thing is change.

Living or Dying Well

Another concept is that clients who are seriously ill need to establish whether they want to live or die. Whatever they choose is not to be judged; it is all right, it is their choice. They should be helped to either live or die in the very best way possible, and have the most joy and fun in doing either.

Many elderly clients with serious diseases, such as advanced cancer, just don't feel that they have any energy left in them to try to get better. In such cases we proceed to discuss what the fun things may be, the dreams, fantasies, or goals that they would like to experience and accomplish before they die. In doing so, some have again felt the joy for life and decided they wanted to live, then did live many more years than anyone expected.

It is important for people to know that they have a choice between living and dying, that the choice is theirs. The practitioner and healer must hone his or her skills to inspire and influence clients to want to live.

Illness as "a Friend"

Most people view their illness as an enemy, something very negative, something to vanquish and eliminate. We need to think about illness as a "friend" who has come to give us a critical warning and help because we have abused our body to the point of developing a disease. This is very difficult to believe, and it might at first sound absurd. However, many people have recovered from serious illnesses as soon as they shifted their thinking and truly believed this to be true.

The condition, or disease (the friend, not foe), forces us to deliberate on our lives and ask ourselves pointed questions. Have I been abusing myself, even subconsciously? Have I extended myself too far? Do I have unresolved relationships? Am I harboring anger, resentment, guilt or fear? Am I trying to help others too much, not taking or making time for myself? Do I need to boost my self-esteem and confidence? Am I on the path of life that truly gives me pleasure and fulfillment? Could I have developed a more serious disease? These and many other questions need to be faced honestly.

Viewing illness as an enemy that must be defeated is a confrontational approach which causes qi to fight back, and this can complicate the situation as in the case with modern drugs. Drugs frequently are used to suppress symptoms, or to "kill" something, such as bacteria. They may do so, but many times they also suppress the immune system and other positive functions in our bodies leading to side reactions with which all of us are familiar. This internal battle may even lead to the development of another condition or disease which is worse than the original.

When lecturing I like to use a maneuver that illustrates the difference in the energy response from both the "confrontional enemy" and "friend" standpoints. The largest, strongest looking man in the audience is selected and invited to come up on the stage. I ask him to place one foot well behind his body, and brace himself in his strongest stance as I try to push him backwards.

If I simply try to push him, confronting him with all my might, I can't move him. However, if I listen to and sense where his qi is, and take a breath with the diaphragm, I can move him backwards quite readily, even though he may outweigh me by as much as 200 pounds. (My students also learn to do this easily.)

In a similar manner, if you fight your illness, the enemy will fight back. If you look upon an illness as a friend who has come to give you a warning, your friend will be very happy to leave when you learn and begin to practice what your friend wants you to know. Do things for yourself; treat your body, mind and spirit better; resolve the anger; repair relationships, etc., and the friend will leave. It is amazing how just changing that one attitude can produce miraculous improvement.

The Child Within

One theory of The Chow System is that there is a child within us, that each part of our body is a child within itself, and we need to look at the body from that standpoint. If we think of each part of our body as a child, then when that part improves to any degree, that child has behaved extremely well (particularly in chronic serious conditions), and is trying to please you "the parent." Just as in true childrearing, you need to affirm that the child has done something correctly, that it is good, and pleases you very much. With that affirmation and appreciation, the child, or that part of your body, will strive to do even better. Without this affirmation, improvements may stop.

Affirmations and The Computer Mind

A corresponding theory goes along with this affirmation. Imagine that your mind is a computer. The more you affirm the child or the healing within you, the more your "computer-mind" will pick up everything that you say and literally try to please you. Whatever you say is captured by your computer-mind, and it will do what you say. If you have a chronic pain condition or illness, and you repeatedly say that you have a pain, or are not feeling well, your computer-mind will act on what you say and amplify that negative condition because it thinks that is what you want. Over time it will continue to compute and intensify the pain program, the illness program.

When you cut that cycle with positive affirmations and a statement of improvements, the computer-mind suddenly realizes: "Oh, you really don't want to have pain. You have been talking about pain all the time, or illness all the time, and that is what I thought you wanted." You need to re-program the computer-brain to say, "I want to feel better." Instead of stating a problem you have, you need to state how you *want* to feel. For example you can say, "I want to feel better," or, "I need to work harder to feel better," or, "I need to practice my breathing in order to get better," instead of saying, "It is so hard to breathe with the diaphragm. I can't breathe that way." When you state the problem, always follow up with a positive statement of what you need to do to improve. Eventually you will get to the point where you don't need to state your problem and can just state the expression of how you want your body to feel. People with long term chronic conditions find this is difficult because of ingrained habits, and they must work diligently to change them. This applies to healthy people who wish to excel as well.

Only with the application of these philosophical and supportive measures, and others yet to come, will the actual exercises of Qigong be truly *essential* Qigong exercises, not what I call *empty* Qigong exercises.

Peace Within Yourself

Part of the healing process involves being at peace with yourself and others. It is important to settle conflicts with parents, brothers, sisters, friends, other family members or associates, etc. If problems are complex, and would take too much time and energy to resolve, the best action is to simply let them go. Forgive and/or ask for forgiveness. Meditation and Qigong can help in this process. It is not necessary to spend excessive time analyzing and re-analyzing past experiences. Unresolved conflicts can upset balance and harmony in the body, as well as in the environment.

People need to decide what they really want, to realize that despite what may have occurred in the past, we still have choices of what we want to do in the future. Look to the future and make constructive plans.

Secrets

There are happy, joyful secrets, but also fearful ones. Harboring deep, dark, fearful secrets constricts qi, which in turn affects the body, mind, and spirit and can make a person ill. Secrets don't need to be divulged to just anyone, but we need to have friends (at least one) in whom we can confide. Inability to confide in a friend may indicate a fear of appearing ridiculous and unacceptable, which in turn can lower self esteem. Most times, by confiding in the right person, a heavy burden or fear will be relieved. Often we wonder why we didn't do so sooner.

Dreams and Fantasies

Having dreams and fantasies is important because they open our qi to feelings of freedom of expression. Some people want to believe they are "realistic," and realistic people often think that fantasies can't come true. Perhaps they don't express or aspire to fantasies, fearing disappointment. Or they may be blamed for having their "head in the clouds." All of this affects not only how people respond to life situations, but it also affects the ability of the body to initiate a healing response. Fearing how people think about us can adversely affect our qi, as demonstrated in energy testing. Being able to dream and fantasize can help the creative spirit and healing power. It can facilitate the visualization process in meditation. It can help you reach goals you never thought possible. Remember the song, "To Dream the Impossible Dream."

Drawings

Clients may be asked to make colored crayon drawings of themselves, other people, and events in their lives. These drawings often reveal deep feelings about personalities and life styles, and indicate if energy channels are open or constricted. They can convey both good or bad images in one picture.

People with low self esteem sometimes draw themselves as tiny, black, stick people. Troubled children may draw themselves off in a corner, isolated from other family members. Dr. Bernie Siegle likes to show a drawing from a cancer patient who was advised by her doctor to have chemotherapy. The devil is shown approaching the patient with a huge needle and syringe. Such drawings apparently reveal feelings from a deep subconscious level of awareness.

Pictures may vary greatly. Some people create abstract forms depicting movement and emotions. Sometimes pictures can show a person blossoming into a positive space. Some pictures may be very subtle and skill is needed in their proper interpretation.

THEORIES OF TRADITIONAL CHINESE MEDICINE

This section will touch briefly on some of the theories of Traditional Chinese Medicine, upon which Qigong is based. Theories of TCM generally sound quite strange to people who encounter them for the first time. If you already are familiar with the theories of TCM, you can skip this brief introduction. If you are not familiar with TCM theories, you may find them of interest, but please don't dwell on them, or become confused. There are many good books on theories of TCM and a few are listed in the bibliography. There are also many good seminars on this including ones held by the Qigong Institute, East West Academy of Healing Arts. An introduction to the simpler aspects of these theories is helpful in learning the beginning exercises of The Chow Integrated Healing System, and Qigong.

TCM is founded upon the Daoist theory, which means the "right way of life." Daoist theory assumes that a person is born with everything necessary for life, that we start life being perfect and in harmony with nature. It also teaches that we must treat life preciously by eating right, sleeping right, acting right, and respecting everything around us, for we are connected with the Universe.

Energy Points and Meridian Channels

One of the best known theories of TCM is that invisible energy channels or meridians run throughout our bodies (and through the bodies of all living things). There are twelve major bilateral meridians, two other singular ones that go up and down the midline of the body, and many others. Qi travels through these meridians in a known pattern. Located along these meridians are over 600 energy points which can be stimulated or sedated in different ways to affect the energy system. In addition, there are hundreds of other energy points that are not located on meridians.

Meridians are named after body organs or functions, such as the Heart, Small Intestine, Spleen/Pancreas, Stomach, Lung, Large Intestine, Kidney, Bladder, Liver, Gall Bladder, Pericardium, and Triple Warmer. The meridians refer not only to the organs after which they are named, but also to correspondences according to the Law of The Five Elements.

These meridians and points were identified between 2,000 and 3,000 thousand years ago. In modern times the system has been verified in studies with electronic instruments, as well as with radioisotopes. When an isotope is injected into an energy point, it can be tracked and found to travel up or down a channel according to the direction of flow indicated in ancient charts. However, according to Western medicine, the meridians do not correspond to any known anatomic structures such as veins, arteries, nerves, or lymphatics.

According to some texts, energy points are about two millimeters in diameter and skin resistance at an energy point is markedly reduced. Therefore, points can easily be found with instruments that can detect a change in skin resistance.

Another way of demonstrating energy systems is through the use of Kirlian photography, which was developed in Russia. A coronal effect occurs when the hands and feet are placed on film and exposed to 25,000 volts emanating from a Tesla transformer (at very low amperage). Scientists contest exactly what is being recorded on

Figure 1. Kirlian photo showing energy patterns surrounding four finger tips of the right hand of a person suffering from hay fever. The heavy black appearance of the patterns displays an excessive accumulation of energy.

the photograph, but nobody doubts that the method can show changes in energy patterns from the use of drugs, mood changes, acupuncture, or various other treatments. Photos can be taken of the fingers, toes or other body parts, before a treatment or exercise of some kind. After the treatment another photo is taken to see if the patterns have changed.

Dr. Thelma Moss, formerly of the University of California , Los Angeles, has done some of the highest quality and most publicized work in Kirlian photography (in the 1970s). Dr. Moss liked

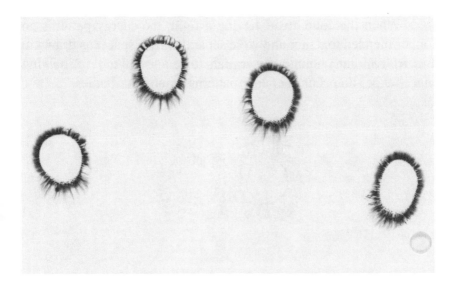

Figure 2. Kirlian photo taken a few minutes after energy points were stimulated with acupuncture needles. Coronal patterns show a lower concentration of energy (Photos courtesy of F. Fuller Royal M.D.).

to show two photographs which are depicted in drawings below. Kirlian photographs were taken of the index fingers of a married couple when everything was going well in their relationship. Energy patterns around the fingers blended together as shown in Figure 3.

Figure 3. Drawing representing one of Dr. Moss' photos showing the energy patterns around index fingers of a married couple during a period of compatibility.

When the couple was having a fight, the energy patterns no longer blended together and were separated by a space, as drawn in Figure 4. Kirlian photography appears to be a useful tool in showing that changes do occur in energy patterns around our bodies.

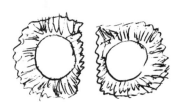

Figure 4. Drawing representing one of Dr. Moss' photos showing the energy patterns of the same couple during a severe conflict.

Dr. Moss also recorded the Kirlian effect in color on videotapes. In one tape a person placed the side of his face against the plate. Energy points were shown clearly and looked like twinkling stars. The points were located exactly where they were drawn in records from China that are over 2,000 years old.

In another videotape, the patterns of all ten fingers were shown of a man who had injured his left wrist. Halo patterns around the fingers of the left hand were very small; those around the right hand very large. Acupuncture needles were placed in energy points to treat his injury. Over the next twenty seconds, halo patterns surrounding fingers of the left hand grew: patterns around the fingers on the right hand shrank, until all finger patterns were of equal size and appearance. Everyone in the audience felt he or she had witnessed visually what people in China had been theorizing about for 3,000 years.

Another method of demonstrating that an energy system is functioning in the body is through muscle testing. Examples of this are presented in Chapters 6 and 8.

Law of The Five Elements and a Microcosm/Macrocosm Concept

This universal connection is exemplified by the theory of the Law of The Five Elements (fire, earth, metal, water, wood) in which each so called "element" is an emblem for a category of related functions and qualities. Our organs have many correspondences that represent the entirety of nature and the Universe. The concept of Microcosm and Macrocosm signify that each of us is a part of a larger cosmic whole, the Universe. Each organ, and each cell in our body is a replica of the whole. This concept is exemplified in the Law of The Five Elements.

Many correspondences are involved, but the most interesting and common ones are that every organ is related to an element, an emotion, a sound, a taste, a color, a particular other part of the body, an animal, a smell, certain seasons and climates, and time of day.

These correspondences in the Law of The Five Elements theory indicate to us that minute things in our daily lives influence our health, immune system, and well-being. For example, an individual may be fairly easy going, but for a few days or a week he or she may become very easily annoyed and angered and has no patience. The Five Element theory of correspondences would indicate that the Liver and Gall Bladder qi must be imbalanced because anger is the emotion of the Liver. People with this imbalance would choose to wear green colored clothes and select sour food without knowing why.

Another example would be if a person is experiencing some loss, sadness or grief, loss of hair, or changes in skin texture. This pattern is indicative of an imbalance of Lung or Large Intestine qi because these signs are related to those organs. This person can be observed to have a craving for spicy or tart food and to choose to wear white clothes.

The Law of The Five Elements theories are very complex and exciting. If you wish to pursue these concepts further, references can be found in the Bibliography.

Balance and Harmony of Qi Equals Health

Another theory is that a balance and harmony of qi essentially means good health. Initial disharmony and imbalance or blockage of qi are indicative of what I refer to as "dis-ease" of body, mind, and spirit, which may lead to full blown diseases if the person is not capable of coping with these early imbalances.

These concepts, along with others, have practical value because they assist in making a diagnosis of the energy disturbance that is causing an illness. After a TCM diagnosis has been made of the energy imbalance, practitioners of TCM apply treatment steps that are designed to re-establish a balance and harmony of qi in the body. Thus, a healthy state is regained.

Yin and Yang

In TCM theory everything in the entire Universe is classified as being either Yin or Yang, the concept of Dual Forces. For example, Yin signifies female, negative, dark, deep, concave, inner, and introverted. Yang is male, positive, bright, surface, convex, outer, and extroverted. Other distinguishing factors are hot/cold, and excess/deficient. None of these terms means good or bad, even though this may appear to be the case.

Yin and Yang must co-exist in harmony and in proper proportion for us to be healthy. The underlying concept of TCM is the necessity of keeping these two forces Yin and Yang in balance.

TCM Theories About Nutrition

Nutrition is of the utmost importance because, in addition to energy we receive from air, food is the major fuel for the body. You are what you think, and you are what you eat as well. Many theories of TCM relate to food. For a thorough discussion of these concepts, I recommend books translated by Dr. Henry Lu.

In TCM, disease conditions are classified as being either Yin and Yang, (the Yin referring to deficient energy, Yang being excess energy), and food is categorized accordingly. Generally, meats are Yang, and vegetables are Yin. There are also categories Yin within Yang, Yang within Yin, Yin within Yin, and Yang within Yang.

Foods can be classified by color as well. Among Yang foods, the reddest of meats are more Yang. As the color of a meat becomes lighter, it becomes more Yin, such as chicken and turkey. Fish with darker flesh such as red salmon are more Yang. Fish with white flesh are more Yin.

Green leafy vegetables are the most Yin of all foods. Vegetables that grow up toward the heavens are Yin because "Heavenly Father" is Yang, and opposites attract. "Mother Earth" is Yin, so vegetables that grow into the ground are Yang.

Yin conditions include diarrhea, thin nasal discharge, thin sputum, tired eyes, and a feeling that we want to sleep because we don't have any energy. Yin conditions rarely are associated with a fever.

In Yang conditions there is an excess of energy. We want to run, have a fever, a parched throat, a dry hacking cough, and might have fever and chills alternating back and forth, hot and cold. With Yang conditions we can have spells where we don't have enough energy, then swing back to Yang-excess.

Logic would dictate that in a Yang condition treatment may involve an excess of Yin foods, but this is not so. Yes, we should eat primarily more Yin food than Yang, but some Yang food is included. The Chinese diet is based on moderation, and does not allow excesses. Excesses can cause unbalanced qi.

Growing up in a traditional Chinese household, children learned what kind of food was beneficial for what condition. We often heard sayings such as, "Eat this because it is good for your eyes; eat this because it is good for your skin; eat this because it is good for your hair; eat this because it is good for your energy; eat this because it is summer and you need to reduce the fire a bit; eat this in the winter because you need to increase your fire; or eat this because you need to increase moisture because it is too dry."

The ritual of eating is important as well. The Chinese eat at a round table and food is served family style in the center. Each person has his or her own bowl of rice, but the main dishes all are shared. In the Chinese household congeniality, consideration, and respect for people who are older is exemplified. I recall that each child in the family had to bid each person in the family to eat, before they started eating themselves. We had to identify each family member by name from the eldest to the youngest, not in a random order. The elders spoke first, then the younger. Certainly nobody ate unless they first politely bid everyone else to begin to eat.

In a more formal setting, people never just help themselves to the food, as do most Westerners. They always offer to help others with food before they help themselves, even though they see that the other person's plate already is laden with food. Before they take a second helping, they always offer food to others.

The Chinese diet is primarily composed of vegetables, plus small portions of meat that are pre-cut into small pieces. Only after the arrival of Western influence did Chinese people begin to serve chunks of meat and big pieces of food. Food was always cut into small, dainty, bite sized pieces, because cutting food at the table is considered to be barbaric. Chop sticks are viewed as being extensions of the fingers, so when you eat you are picking up your food daintily with extensions of your fingers.

When applied in combination with other measures, these concepts and philosophies help to balance qi. Although sounding strange at first, they have been used successfully to activate the body's intuitive healing process. As you progress into Chapters 6 and 7, keep these concepts and philosophies in mind as you learn more about this system of Qigong.

Chapter 6: ENHANCING QIGONG PRACTICE

"My life is in my hands, not in the control of heaven and earth."
Laozi

APPLYING THE CHOW INTEGRATED HEALING SYSTEM

The best way to learn The Chow System is to participate in one of Dr. Chow's brief training sessions. As this will not be possible for the majority of readers, a learning sequence is presented that can produce excellent results, as well as minimize side effects. We advise that you begin by reviewing all of the material in this book before attempting to begin any exercises or other measures described.

The first thing to do is to concentrate on gaining an understanding of the basic concepts in TCM, briefly described in Chapter 5. Then begin to practice proper posture and breathing with the diaphragm, as described below. The next step is to begin to meditate for a week or two. A meditation tape is available. Other supportive measures described in this chapter can be incorporated into your daily routine during this time. Begin to practice the Qigong exercises themselves (described in Chapter 7) after you have practiced these supportive measures for about two weeks.

The following text by Dr. Chow contains the supportive measures of The Chow Integrated Healing System.

Spectacular healing can occur with Qigong practice alone. However, where stress is more prevalent and life styles more complex, Qigong practice *plus* other supportive measures are necessary to achieve the same results. For instance, in China, life is more simple. People are more likely to follow good health habits than we are in the West. Most of their food is fresh, not processed. In most areas they are not exposed to chemical agents used on food or by industry.

Most people in China continue to follow life style patterns which are built into their culture. There are daily routines based in Daoist philosophy in which there are correct ways to breathe, walk, eat, think, behave, etc. The family unit in general, continues to be strong. All these things help to reduce levels of stress. Unfortunately, many of these habits are beginning to change rapidly as China follows more patterns from the West.

In the West, life is far more complex. There is much concern over work situations, interpersonal relationships, status, etc. There is less support from the extended family and the community. One's role is less clear than in China. There is more general and industrial pollution. Health practices are poorer.

If people in the West want to gain optimal benefits from the practice of Qigong, it is important that they change many of their unhealthy habits. I also stress the importance of continuing to practice Qigong and the following supportive measures all through your life. The power of doing so is exemplified in the examples of people with serious illnesses who have experienced miraculous recoveries from their illnesses.

PROPER POSTURE AND DIAPHRAGMATIC BREATHING

Proper posture is important to proper breathing. Stand or sit up straight, using the spine as a support. Visualize that a Silver Thread extends from the ground up through the inside of the tailbone (energy point Governing Vessel #1), up the spine, to the top point of the head (the bai wei point, Governing Vessel #20, the Point of 100 Reasons).

To find the bai wei energy point, look straight ahead; draw a line from both ears where they join the head to the top of the head. Then draw a line from a point between the eyebrows (the third eye) to the middle of the ridge at the back of your head (the occiput). Where the lines cross at the top of the head is the bai wei. At birth this is the soft spot, or fontanelle. Feeling the stretch of your spine in keeping the center Silver Thread taut, move your shoulders back and down. Let everything else hang loosely around the center Silver Thread.

Keep your body still and calm. From the seat of life (dantian-- located 2 inches below the navel and 1 inch inward), visualize a Silver Thread that pulls straight forward from you, tilting your pelvis forward just slightly, so that your upper torso fits properly into the pelvis. This is your proper position. Proper posture is for all times... standing, sitting, and lying.

Proper breathing is the basis of Qigong and life. In proper diaphragmatic breathing, it is not necessary to move the upper chest or the shoulders at all. Just below the lower end of the sternum (breast bone) is the diaphragm area, or upper abdomen. Keeping everything else still and in proper posture, physically move the upper abdomen/diaphragm area out and in, out and in, slowly. The expansion and contraction of the chest walls and diaphragm create a vacuum which automatically moves air in and out of the body.

For inhalation, physically extend the upper abdomen/diaphragm area, and move the chest walls outward to expand the chest cavity, allowing room for the lungs to expand. Air will automatically enter the lungs through the nostrils if you keep your lips closed. For exhalation, physically move the upper abdomen/diaphragm area in, forcing the lungs to push air out in a small steady stream through the lips.

Lifting the shoulders and chest walls to initiate breathing is an unnatural, bad habit we learn as we grow. In chest breathing we pull our shoulders up and tense the muscles of the neck and shoulders. This creates what I call a sense of a paranoic posture and mentality... the feeling that we must be on guard, on the defensive. When we let our shoulders drop, we feel relaxed.

Raising the shoulders and pulling the back and neck up tightens muscles in those areas, causing muscle spasms. Major energy meridians, particularly the Bladder meridians, pass through these areas. According to concepts of TCM, constricting a meridian creates muscle spasms and pain anywhere up and down the entire route of the meridian. The bilateral Bladder meridian starts near the inner angle of the eye, passes over the top of the head, goes down the back and legs and ends in the small toe. The Bladder meridian is a large one on which all other meridians have a connecting point. Therefore, any constriction of this meridian can cause imbalances in other meridians. Thus, simply by breathing with the chest and shoulders, you may create pain in the weakest area of your body. For example, the pain will be in your lower back if that is the weak spot, in your knee if that is the weakest area, and so forth. If the head is the weakest area, you may get a headache. If there is organ weakness, a problem may manifest itself there.

Diaphragmatic breathing should become a regular, natural form of breathing. Newborn babies naturally breathe with the diaphragm. Diaphragmatic breathing is a necessity for professional singers. However, proper breathing can be attained only with proper posture and enough practice.

It has been said that the alveolar capillaries, if laid end to end, would cover an entire tennis court. Proper breathing expands the lungs more fully, facilitating oxygenation and the elimination of carbon dioxide and toxins. These processes are critical to the general health of the body. Frequently a change to proper breathing has by itself corrected many chronic health problems.

PROPER POSTURE, WALKING, AND SITTING

Posture, whether in walking, sitting, or standing, can have serious effects on energy balance. Good posture strengthens qi. Poor posture weakens qi and can cause innumerable problems.

Good posture begins with the head. In proper posture the head is carried quite vertically above the shoulders. From a side view, the ear canals line up over the middle of the shoulders. The head is never projected forward ahead of this line.

The shoulders remain in a pulled back position. Allowing them to rotate to the front of the chest forms an abnormal convex shape in the back. The arms hang loosely so that the space between the thumb and the forefinger face to the front. Besides the Silver Thread holding you in an upright posture, imagine an additional Silver Thread extending from the dantian straight forward to help with smoother walking movements. The pelvis is slightly rotated to the front with the seat tucked in. Do not tighten muscles as that can cause pain. The knees stay slightly flexed, not locked tight. With each step, the foot lands softly and flat on the floor, not toe first, nor heel first. Instead of bouncing up and down when walking, glide and let the knees work as shock absorbers to protect the spine from being jarred.

Practice walking, even running, as if you are carrying a tray of champagne glasses on your head without spilling them. The toes point forward when walking and the arms swing naturally in opposition to the legs. When the right leg moves forward, the left arm moves forward.

When sitting, avoid sliding down in the chair. A ninety degree angle is maintained between the thighs and spine. When getting up from a sitting position, first move forward to sit on the front one-third of the chair. Then place one foot under the edge of the chair and the other in front to have the heel of the front foot even with the instep of the back foot and with the feet about three inches apart.

When rising from the chair let the Silver Thread pull you straight up. Go down straight from the standing into a sitting position. When moving to the back or front of a chair maintain an "L" shape between your back and thighs. Always sit in proper posture. After practicing this routine, it will seem very normal, more comfortable, and you will look more regal. Most people try to sit directly back into the back of the chair. This and poor footing strains the back and can create many different types of body aches and pains, particularly in the back itself.

With practice, good posture becomes more natural. Most people find they become very uncomfortable if they revert to their former poor posture. They also become very aware of other people's posture and even begin to help others make improvements. Remember to breathe with the diaphragm at all times. Breathing is everything!

CHOW'S SILVER THREAD, LAW OF THE FIVE ELEMENTS MEDITATION

Introductory Comments

Next to posture and breathing correctly with the diaphragm, meditation is probably the most important supportive practice in the development of our qi. This meditation process has been tested and found to be very subtle, yet powerful. There are many other good methods of meditation, but this one was developed as part of a larger system of knowledge in correspondence with the Law of The Five Elements. It is used in The Chow System for relaxation, reinforcement, assessment, and therapeutics.

This meditation process serves many purposes:

1) To improve breathing and posture.
2) To assess health status.
3) To promote health and healing in oneself and others.
4) To manage stress and pain.
5) To increase general stamina.
6) To change lifestyles in a positive way.

The degree of effectiveness of these measures depends upon regular practice. Ultimately each of us must become aware that only we have the responsibility of taking charge of our lives.

This meditation is an integral part of courses taught in The Chow System of qi energy and touch healing. Other important components are Qigong and Taiji exercises (a moving meditation), and good sound nutritional principles based upon Chinese theories of Yin and Yang.

People who do not fully learn how to handle qi properly have experienced adverse reactions. Proper posture, breath, meditation, visualization, Qigong and Taiji exercises are some of the best things people can do to prevent adverse reactions from occurring and to discipline energy and maximize their own power.

Hopefully, this particular meditation process teaches us to respect the tremendous power of a universal life-force. This life-force can be a great ally or a devastating foe. It should be well respected, not abused. People refer to this energy or life-force as God, the Greater Spirit, Buddha, or whatever deity or expression you feel most closely associated. We all are speaking of the same ultimate power source, but from different tongues and cultural perspectives.

For convenience, the terms life-force and qi will be used in this meditation instruction. It is important for you to use this qi with love and great care for the good of humanity, not for greed and selfish desire.

The first three stages in this meditation are presented here. Stages four and five are more advanced meditations for projecting healing and are not presented here.

Stage 1) The centering of oneself.
Stage 2) Calling upon the universal life-force and power represented by the Five Elements to enhance the qi within oneself.
Stage 3) Cleansing, or clearing and healing of oneself.

It is necessary to follow the stages of meditation in the order presented, particularly while you are learning. Also, if you are already familiar with another method, please practice this method for now and don't mix two systems together. Give this practice a serious chance for at least three to six months, then assess its value to you. Practice twenty minutes twice daily, morning and afternoon or evening, until it becomes second nature, as automatic as breathing.

The process will promote and maintain proper breathing and posture. This practice is in addition to the time you devote to Qigong exercises.

As you become proficient, you will require less time to go through each of the stages. Once you have learned the meditation well, you will immediately be able to recall the stage you need: you will automatically and quickly move through the necessary stages.

Students are instructed to "Keep those images and impressions in your computer-mind." This allows you to be able to instantly recall that feeling of being centered, balanced, cleansed, etc., without having to go through a lengthy process each time. The secret is in faithful daily practice.

With proficiency you will also begin to use your own expressions in your meditation, for this is intended to assist you in getting started. However, the stages and the process of how to sit, breathe, use correct posture, etc., are all important to maintain even if you shorten the length of time you meditate or use different expressions.

There are certain laws of nature we need to abide by in the system. Remember, you were born perfect with every possible potential, in every sense in harmony with nature. Also remember that every other person has been born with all possible potential and also is perfect. Everyone should exist in harmony and respect with one another. Enjoy the development of your own strength: your greatest power is your ability to be a catalyst and help others to maximize their abilities.

The ultimate goal for the practice of meditation is to reach a constant state of centeredness, or balanced harmony. You then will have the power to cope more effectively and efficiently with the challenges and stresses of everyday life. With this harnessed power you also can be a more effective healer. Your very PRESENCE and ESSENCE of "BEING" (body, mind, and spirit) can create an environment in which healing will take place.

First Stage of Meditation

The full or half-Lotus position is the ideal position for meditation because energy flows best through what is called the "figure eight" pattern. However, most people need to practice and slowly build up to be able to assume this position. To begin, you can sit on the floor with the aid of a small cushion under your buttocks, then cross your legs in a comfortable position.

It is important to begin in a comfortable position in order to be able to concentrate well. If, because of any medical or physical reasons, you must sit in a chair, place both feet squarely on the ground or floor to maximize circulation of qi. Try to sit up straight and not rest your spine on the back of the chair.

Figure 1. Half-Lotus position, front view.

Now, the half-Lotus position...(Do a full Lotus if possible).

First find a comfortable sitting position on the floor. Try to place your right foot under your left buttock and your left foot over the top of your right thigh (This is the best, but if more comfortable, you can reverse the leg positions). You may not be able to do this at first, but do the best you can, and improve your position gradually.

Figure 2. Half-Lotus position, side view.

Visualize that a Silver Thread is being pulled taut, straight upward from the ground, through your tail bone and up the spine through Governing Vessel #20 (an energy point on the top of the head) and on up to heaven. Posture yourself in response to the upward pull this Silver Thread exerts from the sky. Position your head so your chin is at a ninety degree angle to the ground and your eyes are looking straight ahead at eye level. Your head should not be bowed down, or turned upward.

Now, imagine and feel a second Silver Thread coming from the "Seat of Life" (dantian, which is located two inches below the navel and one inch inward), pulling straight forward. One Silver Thread is pulling your spine upward into good alignment and posture, the other is tilting your pelvis slightly forward so the torso of your body is sitting into your pelvis properly.

Roll your shoulders backward and downward. Keeping the central Silver Thread taut and in place, attach a Silver Thread to each shoulder and drop the threads downward toward the ground to relax the shoulders. If any other part of you feels tense, attach a Silver Thread to that body part and visualize that the thread is pulling it gently down toward the ground. You should feel as if your entire body is being pulled upward by the central Silver Thread which is extending down from above. Keep your shoulders and chest still.

Now breathe deeply with your diaphragm, concentrating on the in and out movement of your diaphragm. Allow the movement of the diaphragm to give your lungs the space to breathe and maximize the capacity of your lungs.

Bring your hands in front of you about one inch forward from the body at the dantian level. Place the palms over one another, about one inch apart, with the palm laogong points facing up (The location of the laogong points in the palms can be found on page 106). Men place the right hand under the left, women the left hand under the right.

Imagine that you have a lemon in each underarm area. Let your arms hang loosely like a suspension bridge from your shoulders. Your forearms are parallel to the floor. As your qi builds, you may feel a "qi field" between your hands. A buffer of qi may develop under your forearms supporting them in place with no effort on your part. It is common for the arms to feel so light they seem to float or disappear. In fact, your entire body might also feel that way.

Realize how potent this qi is and how every little gesture facilitates the strength or weakness of qi. This is illustrated in the energy testing exercises and in the encircling of qi through the body.

Even the placement of the laogong points is important.

During inhalation the tip of your tongue should lightly touch the roof of your mouth just behind the ridge where the upper teeth meet the upper gum. Drop the tongue slightly when breathing out. Create a hollow in the back of your throat. The larger the hollow feels without straining the throat muscles, the more relaxed the jaw will be. The relaxation of your jaws automatically will cause the rest of your body to relax.

Relax all of your muscles by letting them drop physically and mentally, allowing your whole body to hang loosely from the central Silver Thread. Let all of the muscles in your face relax. Relax the eye muscles, then gently close your eyes. Continue breathing with the diaphragm, slowly and deeply.

Qi moves from the dantian to all parts of the body through the "Microcosmic Cycle" and three "gateways" located in the low back, chest, and neck. As you inhale, visualize qi moving from your dantian down to the pubic area, around to the tail bone, then up your spine (along the Governing Vessel meridian) behind the Silver Thread, up the lower back, upper back and neck, over the top of the head to the roof of the mouth. As you exhale, qi flows back down the front central line of the body (the Conception Vessel meridian) returning to the dantian. This is referred to as the Microcosmic Cycle of breath. The flow of qi through this pathway should be continuous.

This vibrant qi moves through every muscle, tendon, bone, and the trillions of cells in your body. With every complete breath, your qi is enhanced and maximized, giving you infinitely more power.

Now you breathe and relax in a manner that is strengthening your own potential. If thoughts come to mind, just acknowledge them and let each go. Don't try to make your mind blank or a little black box, for that will be forcing your thought process. Just acknowledge each thought that flows through and let it go. Soon all thoughts will have come and gone and you will reach a state of just being.

If there are noises, pleasant or unpleasant, acknowledge each noise and let it flow out. Soon the noises will seem to disappear or become a background for your meditation, faint and distant.

Let yourself experience fully whatever it is you are feeling, whether it is physical, emotional, spiritual, pleasant or unpleasant. Don't try to avoid any unpleasant feelings; these also need expression. Experience all of these feelings, both good and bad, to their fullest. Keep them in your computer-mind. Often problems may become resolved from the depth of your subconscious, without a conscious awareness of the process. Feel the warmth flow through your body, the relaxed muscles free from tension and stress, the calmness .... If you experience anything other than what has been said here, acknowledge it. Let yourself feel and appreciate it fully.

You might see or feel colors, you might feel a fusing with the energy around you, your body may experience movement ... a swaying with the atmospheric energy around you. Let yourself flow with it... feel the peace ... feel the oneness. Let yourself respond to your body's need for expression, whether in sound or action. It's good to be spontaneous. If you are in a group, do not be disturbed by actions and sounds of others. People respond in many different ways in meditation and this is perfectly all right.

Second Stage of Meditation

Having so centered and maximized your own energy, now call upon the universal energy forces that exist around us...the greater forces that are there for you to call upon and use. The Universe is represented here by the Five Elements: fire, earth, metal, water, and wood. Think about each of these elements in order. Let yourself feel all the impressions and images that come to mind. Take your time. Don't force images or impressions upon yourself. Let it evolve.

Think of FIRE .... the images and impressions of FIRE, keeping them in your computer-mind for one minute.

Think of EARTH .... the images and impressions of EARTH, keeping them in your computer-mind for one minute.

Think of METAL .... the images and impressions of METAL,
        keeping them in your computer-mind for one minute.
Think of WATER .... the images and impressions of WATER,
        keeping them in your computer-mind for one minute.
Think of WOOD .... the images and impressions of WOOD,
        keeping them in your computer-mind for one minute.

Let yourself acknowledge how it feels now that you have connected with the universal energy life forces and called upon their power to reinforce your own to enhance the essence of your own existence...your being. The **essence** of your being is the true healing factor for yourself or for others. Your very **presence** can make another person feel infinitely better without having done anything to the person. Let yourself acknowledge and appreciate this power within yourself.

Third Stage of Meditation

Moving through the third stage of meditation cleanses or clears yourself of any blockage, tension, and/or problem which may exist in you, to heal yourself. These may be of body/mind and/or spirit in nature and in any degree of intensity.

Envision the problem as an unbalanced or affected energy in any image you wish...something unpleasant you want to move out of your body...for example a gray cloud, a dark smoke, sharp needles, barbs, etc. Just let the image come. At the same time, move healthy vibrant qi from the dantian directly to fill that area. See or feel the affected qi move directly out of your body from that area and dissipate into the atmosphere, actually disappearing right into thin air. Do not move affected energy to any other area of your body, especially not back into the torso, the center of the body, nor to your head; these are vital and extra-sensitive parts of your body. It is very important to move the affected energy straight <u>out</u> from the affected area and visualize it disappearing into the atmosphere.

See that part of your body, whether it be mental, physical or spiritual, as whole, healthy, vibrant and alive. Feel this vibrancy, aliveness, and healthiness. Whatever the image of being healthy is to you, let that image come to mind. Just let this image evolve and come, do not force it. Let the image be beautiful and perfect.

The image may be glowing pink tissues, a white light, a lovely warm feeling, different colors, beautiful flowers, clear water, etc. The body will choose the image(s) or feeling(s) it needs. Let good qi push all the negative energy out. Then spread the beautiful and perfect image throughout your body, mind, and spirit. Become that beautiful and perfect image.

If you have concentrated on a certain part of your body and another part seems to come to mind, that part of you is saying to you, "I need help." So, concentrate on the part of your body that intuitively came to mind, then go back to the part with which you originally wanted to work. If there is no particular part that needs special attention, then just focus on your total body/mind/spirit self.

Feel the vibrant state within you. Feel the harmony, the warmth moving through your body, the muscles, the tendons, the bones, the trillions of cells in your body, all feeling healthy, vibrant, and alive. Feel them all contributing to the total health of you as a unique and marvelous individual human being. Be thankful for this healthy state. Acknowledge and appreciate this feeling. Continue with the clearing/cleansing of yourself until you feel satisfied. Take your own time until you're ready to come out of meditation.

Do not worry if you have unpleasant feelings or temporarily fall asleep. Whatever you experience is what your body needs at this time and moment. You are allowing your body to fulfill this need. The important thing is to experience fully, whatever the sensation.

When you are ready to come out of meditation, concentrate on a few deeper diaphragmatic breaths and enjoy the sense of harmony within yourself. Encircle the universal qi by bringing your arms out to the side, encircling them up and forward, and bring your palms down, right hand outside of the left, towards your dantian with one complete breath. Do this three times, then relax with your palms turned upward on your lap. Slowly open your eyes, enjoying the quiet harmony of being in tune with your environment and the Universe...that powerful feeling of centeredness and health.

POSITIVE MENTAL ATTITUDES

Positive mental attitudes can be shown to strengthen qi and negative attitudes to weaken qi. In turn, this will affect your health: strong qi will strengthen the immune response and other functions of the body, and vice versa. The first step is to affirm positive feelings about yourself, and for this purpose I recommend the following procedure.

In the privacy of your own home, stand in front of the mirror in the nude. Look at yourself from the top of your head to the tip of your toes and like what you see. Say nice things about your body and yourself. Laugh in good humor if you wish. You need to feel good about yourself and love and like yourself to improve your balance of qi, as you will soon see. Think only about positive things. Love and like attributes ordinarily perceived as negatives, such as extra bulges of fat or bald spots. If you like yourself it is more likely that you will attract people to like you as well, and the opposite is true.

Positive attitudes can be demonstrated with muscle testing in the manner presented in a study published by Dr. Sancier and myself, described in Chapter 8. If a person is tested immediately after saying out loud, "**I am strong**," he or she will test strong. If tested immediately after saying, "I am weak," the person will test weak. Bringing even the slightest doubt into the mind will have a weakening effect. If a person says out loud, "I **think** I am strong," he or she will test weak because of the subtle doubt injected into the statement.

Try this experiment with a friend. In a standing position the "testee" holds both arms out in front of the body with the hands at the level of the forehead. The testee places one hand on top of the other, keeping the elbows straight and the mind neutral. The "tester" then presses down on the testee's hands with one hand, applying a steady force for a count of about five seconds. The intent is not to overpower the testee, just to measure strength and the time the force can be successfully resisted. The same amount of force should be applied to the testee's arms on each test.

The tester should not be thinking about anything else but the test and should not anticipate the outcome. He or she should be as neutral as possible. The testee should say with conviction, "**I am strong**," then be tested, and his or her strength noted. Then the testee says, "I **think** I am strong," and is tested again. The last statement made should be a positive one in order not to leave the testee in a weakened condition. Most people can make this testing system work well enough to feel differences in muscle strength. This test may be done for countless situations. If the test does not work for you the first time, don't worry. You may need to be shown how to do it properly.

This simple maneuver shows how we can be governed by our thoughts. People who go through life thinking about all of their problems and how ineffective they are, create a weakening effect in the body. Those who greet each day and challenge with a positive attitude strengthen themselves. Those who think they can't do something usually can't, setting the stage for a self-fulfilling prophecy. People who believe they will not get well interfere with their body's efforts to heal, and probably won't get well.

To turn this around, practice the next exercise to enhance a positive atmosphere, called "news and good."

The Power of Positive Expression

News and good can be practiced by yourself or with others. For example, this exercise is supportive to the family if done at the dinner table when everyone is together. It also is highly useful at the beginning of business or staff meetings.

The rules of the game are simple. Everyone takes a turn sharing a piece of news that is uplifting or positive. This can be something that has happened to them in a personal or business area or something that may affect the entire group. During my Qigong training seminars students frequently told about new things they were experiencing as they progressed with their exercises and meditation. Some responses were related to the alleviation of aches, pains, and headaches, or sensations felt during meditation. Some people have related improvements in relationships with family members and loved ones. Nothing negative or questionably negative is allowed and everyone must contribute. Try it out!

Many people insist they are very positive people but by their attitudes and the way they speak and express themselves they are extremely negative in many subtle ways. An example is when people say, "Why don't we do something?" instead of the more positive, "Let's do something." Again, muscle testing will show weakening with the phrase, "why don't we..."

Many people seem to be unable to make a straightforward positive statement without a qualification. They will say, "I feel better, but I still have a pain." Or, when you ask how they are, they will begin talking about negative things. Human nature is very funny and frustrating that way.

When clients have had obviously good results, such as a definite relief of pain, I ask them how they feel. Often they answer, "Well, I don't think I have the pain now, but I don't know how long I am going to be pain free." They can't bring themselves to say the more positive and simple statement, "I don't have the pain now," or better yet, "I am feeling improved."

Possibly they fear that in making such a hopeful statement, they will be disappointed if the pain returns the next moment. They must realize that if they acknowledge positive responses, they are speaking for that moment only. This improves the chance for long lasting healing. Even the slightest improvement needs to be acknowledged or affirmed. A high degree of skill and sensitivity is needed to observe minute changes that take place.

Some people find making changes extremely difficult, while others surprise us with their flexibility. Those with a sense of humor seem to be able to change more readily because they are more flexible and their qi is more open. If you find that you are unconsciously making negative statements, develop the habit of noticing exactly what you are saying, then immediately correct yourself. Be courageous and don't be afraid of having a good laugh at yourself.

It is necessary for people to know all their own positive qualities, talents, and attributes, and what is good for them. Some people never acknowledge this. This affects their self-esteem. With this in mind, I have clients write out a list of their positive attributes when they are listing their goals and dreams on the first appointment. A person also should be able to discover the positive qualities in others; be able to look another person directly in the eye and compliment him or her on some positive quality.

In thinking or talking about happy thoughts or good news, the topic does not need to be something spectacular. Sometimes little things are the most important. The key is to train ourselves to be able to focus on the positive aspects of any circumstance. When this is done, energy testing can show a strengthening effect.

AT LEAST EIGHT HUGS A DAY AND YOU CAN'T OVERDOSE

Cultural practices of hugging vary widely. In America, most people hug only their spouses or close family members. In many European and Latin American cultures hugging is a common practice, not only between family members, but among close friends. Hugging is not practiced openly in China, where it is not considered good taste to show affection in public. This is unfortunate. Hugging is definitely beneficial, and contagious!

In the fall of 1991, I gave a 100 hour course on Qigong in

Vancouver, B.C. Ten staff members of a nursing home in Washington State took the course on the recommendation of pastor Walter Moris, administrator of the Columbia Lutheran Home in Seattle (where I participated in a research study in 1984, described in Chapter 8). The class had thirty students and eight hugs a day was prescribed as part of the course. Everyone became accustomed to hugging everybody else. After returning home after the first weekend class, students from the nursing home began to try out what they were learning.

One student named Eva reported her problems in working with an elderly patient who always had a negative attitude about everything. Nothing pleased her. Her food was either too hot, cold, spicy or bland. Her bowels never worked normally. Sometimes she refused to swallow her medicine. Does this sound like anyone you know?

One day, after having a particularly difficult time with this woman, Eva decided to try a different approach. The patient was standing at the side of her bed when Eva asked her if she could give her a hug. This perpetually pessimistic woman looked surprised, but didn't decline and received a nice, long hug. The next day when Eva went to work, the woman was standing at the side of her bed waiting for her hug. After that she seldom complained, and caring for her became much easier.

Hugging began to spread throughout the 187 patients and staff at the nursing home. Staff members hugged patients and patients began to hug each other. The general level of communication and friendliness began to improve. Hugging became accepted as a powerful tool in improving relationships.

One day a notice was found on the staff bulletin board that read, "Thank you for not hugging." Although comical, it expressed the true opinion of a male staff member who felt uncomfortable with hugging. When he was offered a hug by a fellow staff member, he leaped back two paces. A few days later he did accept a hug...the sign disappeared a few hours later.

The hug is a powerful therapeutic tool because it breaks down barriers and brings people closer together. The overall effect is to build up and maintain our levels of qi.

Benefits of Hugs and Touch

1) Feeling a sense of caring
2) Being in touch
3) Feeling of being loved
4) Evoking laughter
5) Improving interpersonal relationships
6) Stabilization of vital signs
7) Promotion of healing
8) Increasing the sense of well-being
9) Elevation of mood, morale, possibly even morals
10) Improved self-esteem and worthiness
11) Increased will or desire to perform and accomplish
12) Delaying the aging process
13) In scientific studies has had positive effects on red blood cells, white blood cells, endorphins, and serotonin.

As with most things, there are correct and incorrect ways to hug. Two people should ease into a hug smoothly. The hug should be a total body, friendly, warm bear hug, with the bodies vertical. The hug should not be a tee-pee hug, where the feet are distanced and only shoulders and chest touch. Try the tee-pee type of hug with someone. It gives the impression that the other person is just going through the motions and is not really interested in you. Avoid the opposite type of hug where the lower parts of the bodies are touching but not the top parts. Arms should embrace the other person without rubbing or massaging. The hug should not be rushed. Do not use the hug as an excuse to make advances to another person. Think of the hug as a friendly warm teddy-bear hug.

We all should get at least eight hugs a day and remember, you can't overdose on hugs.

HUMOR AND LAUGHTER

You can't overdose on humor and laughter either! Everyone should have **at least** three deep belly-aching laughs a day. It doesn't matter how this is achieved. Laughter can be a powerful medicine and balancer of qi. It also enhances sexual qi.

Probably the most famous story about the healing power of laughter, is that of the late Norman Cousins as told in his book, *Anatomy of an Illness, as Perceived by the Patient.* Cousins developed "ankylosing spondylitis," a form of rheumatoid arthritis of the spine. Continual pain kept him bedridden. After discovering that Western medicine could offer nothing more for him than pain medicine to suppress symptoms, he arranged for his physician to continue treating him in a hotel room. He found living in the hotel to be less expensive and more private. The food was better and no one was drawing blood from him several times a day.

Cousins decided to begin what he called a "program calling for the full exercise of the affirmative emotions as a factor in enhancing body chemistry." He began to watch old silent movie comedies by the Marx brothers and films of the television show, *Candid Camera.* He found that when he had a good laugh he didn't hurt for a while. His doctor confirmed that these periods of laughter were followed by a temporary reduction in the sedimentation rate in his blood (a general test for inflammation). Cousins combined his laughter program with high doses of vitamin C intravenously (twenty-five grams per day) and slowly made a complete recovery from his illness.

Some people can see only the dark side of events; some routinely see the positive. Is your cup half full or half empty? If you have a hard time seeing the brighter side of life, purchase some joke books and read one or two jokes a day. Ask your friends for funny stories; try to see humor in things happening around you daily. Even simplistic or corny stories and jokes are better than no stories or jokes at all.

DIET AND FOOD PREPARATION

According to an old expression, Chinese people *live to eat.* Chinese cuisine is famous for its variety. It is possible to eat three meals a day for an entire year without repeating a single dish. They say that, when something new is discovered, the Germans want to dissect it, the Americans want to shoot it to the moon, but the Chinese want to eat it. Steps are taken to produce exotic flavorings and sauces that people in the West would consider to be excessive.

The Chinese always have placed a high priority on the freshness of food and preparation techniques that do not disturb subtle energetic properties. The Chinese refer to high quality fresh foods as "living" foods as opposed to "dead" modern processed and refined foods. The traditional Chinese diet always has consisted of more vegetables than meat.

In TCM, the principal concept concerning food is moderation. Many diets can be beneficial but a diet of moderation will suffice unless people are seriously ill.

Coffee should be discontinued because it contains acids that can play a role in causing neuromuscular spasms and pain. People also should avoid the use of alcohol, cigarettes, tobacco in any form, refined sugar, and modified (processed) salt. If they feel they need sweets, they should eat fruit, a little honey or carob, but very little. If a person is very ill, then larger dietary changes are needed. These changes are determined by a diagnosis of qi imbalances.

Because different tastes relate to different organs in the Law of The Five Elements in TCM, the body needs to have a little of each taste to be balanced well; bitterness for the Heart and Small Intestine qi; sweets for Spleen, Pancreas, and Stomach; tart or spicy for the Lung and Large Intestine; salty for Kidney and Bladder; and sour taste for Liver and Gall Bladder. If there is an absence or excess of one of these tastes, the organ may suffer.

I encourage clients to: eat fresh vegetables and fruit primarily, with small portions of white meat, such as turkey, chicken, and fish;

take small quantities of shell fish because they contain too many toxins; consume more whole grains and other high fiber foods; drink at least ten glasses of liquid a day, perhaps six of which should be plain, chlorine-free water. Chlorine affects the immune system and possibly other systems as well. Salads are all right in moderation, but large amounts of raw vegetables and salads are too Yin. Eat at least nine servings of vegetables and fruits per day especially if moderate or serious illnesses are complicating factors.

We all would be wise to consume larger amounts of cruciferous vegetables (of the cabbage family). Cruciferous vegetables were studied for five years at the National Institutes of Health and were found to contain phytochemicals that help prevent cancer. Other studies found that they are of value in building up the immune system, energizing the body in a general way, and preventing heart disease, respiratory problems, and arthritis.

Avoid fried foods and "junk" foods. Hold consumption of dairy products and fats to a minimum. Avoid "dead" food, such as canned/processed/ artificially flavored, colored, and chemically laden products.

Stay away from sweets, chocolate, and other rich foods, cakes, sauces, etc. However, if you have a craving for sweets, and find that you must give in to the craving on rare occasions, try this. Choose the best quality candy and eat it very slowly and with relish to totally appreciate that taste. In doing so, you can satisfy the craving more easily and faster and will end up eating less.

In contrast, if the candy is eaten quickly and with guilt, the craving will continue and you will end up eating more and more "junk" food. If you handle the problem properly, the craving may not return for a long time.

Eating food slowly and chewing it well is conducive to better digestion. Digestion will function more efficiently if you consider eating to be a gracious event rather than a necessity. The digestive process also functions better when food is eaten in the presence of pleasant company and conversation.

I don't believe it is essential for everyone to follow a pattern of eating three meals a day. We would be better off if we listened to what our bodies tell us about when to eat. However, few people do this. Often we stress our bodies by not supplying food when it is needed and forcing food when it is not. Generally, we should eat a good breakfast, a good lunch, and a light dinner. Though not totally verified, eating at night may cause food to turn into stored fat rather than energy.

An example of the benefits of following ancient concepts in food selection and preparation can be found in the health patterns of Hainan Island, China, which Dr. McGee visited twice in 1990. Hainan Island (population 8 million) is located halfway between Hong Kong and Viet Nam, and forms the Gulf of Tonkin. According to 1989 health statistics, cancer and heart disease were not yet found on the list of the ten most common causes of death. The infant death rate is not much higher than in the United States, there are no premature births nor birth defects. Obstetricians take care of newborn babies instead of pediatricians because of the absence problems in newborns.

In Hainan, all food is prepared fresh, directly from the source. Vegetables are sold by farmers from small push-carts. Fish caught in the ocean the night before are displayed swimming in tanks of sea water, and all are sold by ten in the morning. Housewives take fish home swimming in pails of water keeping them alive as long as possible. The same principle applies to animals. If a chicken dinner is planned, the first step is to catch the chicken. Before 1990, there were no markets that sold food in packages, boxes, bags or bottles.

A man in Haikou asked if people in the West ate fish very often. Dr. McGee told him that they eat a fair amount of fish but that much of it has been frozen. The man looked shocked hearing that anyone would ever consider eating a fish that had been frozen.

Chinatowns in the West resemble the wonderful markets of the Orient with live animals and fish and vegetables fresh from the farm. Everyone should experience shopping in a Chinatown: your tastebuds are titillated and your gastric juices are stimulated with the excitement and vitality of everything. In my courses, I try to include a one-day adventure to a Chinatown.

Vitamin, Mineral Supplements, and Herbs

Western medicine has recently acknowledged the health protecting and age-delaying benefits of vitamins and minerals, especially substances with anti-oxidant properties such as vitamins E, C, Beta-carotene, and the trace mineral, selenium. Much of this research has been done in China and the United States. Air pollution and the stresses of life increase our need for these materials and protective levels are larger than even the best diet can provide.

Therefore, it is advisable to take multi-vitamin and mineral supplements, preferably consuming divided amounts with each meal instead of a single one-a-day type of pill. Supplements in the form of gelatin capsules or pills which dissolve easily and quickly are recommended to achieve the goal of total absorption.

Often herbs are necessary initially to aid in rebalancing qi while a person practices Qigong. TCM practitioners begin by making a TCM diagnosis to determine the type or combination of herbs needed for a particular problem. As many as fifteen herbs may be prescribed at one time. In a traditional practice raw herbs are mixed and brewed into a tea at home. Pre-packaged herbs in pill form are available now but from a classical viewpoint a traditional prescription from a proficient herbalist is more likely to be a precise treatment for the condition.

Scanning

People can learn to scan their bodies for indications of unbalanced qi, or areas of stress and tension. It generally is desirable to scan another person but most people are also able to sense their own areas of unbalanced qi.

Begin by rubbing the laogong points together to increase (see page 106) the level of qi and the sensitivity of your hand. Pass your hand over the body about one to two inches above the skin. Sense what the energy coming from the body feels like and if there are differences or variations. Areas with energy disturbances or imbalances will feel different. For example, warmth or coolness may indicate an excess or absence of qi. You may feel many other sensations not only in your hands, but in other parts of your body as well. Any abnormal area needs to be brushed, then rescanned with your hand to see if it has become re-energized or energized.

ACUPRESSURE

Acupressure is another way of enhancing Qigong while students are building up their qi. The following are a few energy points which, when used in combination, can help people in many ordinary circumstances, such as relief of many kinds of pain, muscle tension in the shoulders and anxieties.

If a point is especially painful, this indicates the presence of a congestion in the energy channel. You should continue to work on this point until tenderness in the point decreases. When the tenderness has gone, gently brush the area with your laogong point. Application of acupressure as described here should be used in combination with proper breathing. Remember, breath is everything.

I would like to emphasize that the other Qigong supportive measures presented so far are more important than acupressure. Please don't let a sudden ability to use acupressure distract you from the more important study of Qigong.

1. The Laogong Point and Brushing Qi

The laogong point, or Pericardium 8, is located in the center of each palm. A person who has pains or tension should use the laogong point to brush qi away from the center line of the body. If a person feels tired, weak, and depleted of energy, then brush qi towards the center line of the body as if you are packing it in. It's amazing how easily many pains and tensions respond to this simple procedure.

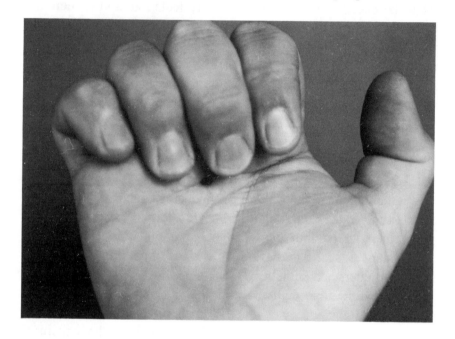

Figure 3. The laogong point is shown at the dot.

2. The Hoku Point, or Large Intestine 4

The hoku point is bilateral and is located between the thumb and index finger. To locate the hoku point, place the flexion crease at the end joint of your right thumb against the web formed by stretching out the thumb and forefinger of the left hand. When you press the right thumb tip down it will be over Large Intestine 4.

The thumb tip should press down on the soft tissue at the base of the angle between the left thumb and forefinger. Don't move off the point once you have found it. Squeezing this area between the right thumb and fingers in the motion of a tiny cyclone may cause some discomfort. It may also produce a tingle, a slight numbness in the little finger and ring finger and even a tingling up the arm. More sensitive people may even feel this sensation right down to their toes.

Maintain pressure on this point for at least five minutes. Stimulation of the hoku point can improve circulation all through the body. Large Intestine 4 can open up energy and blood circulation in the entire upper body. It is called a power point because it can be used for many problems, such as tooth aches, headaches, tired eyes, tension in the shoulders, scapula (shoulder blade), back and neck pains, tendinitis, sinus and respiratory problems, and pain of any sort from the chest up.

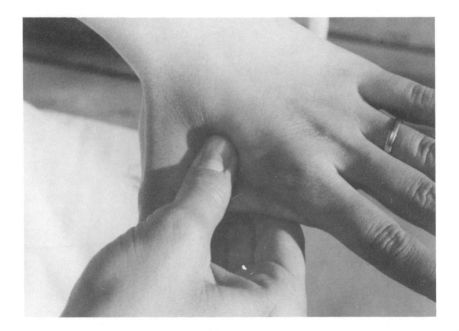

Figure 4. Location of Large Intestine 4.

3. Large Intestine 11

Large Intestine 11 is located at the crease of the elbow. It is found by bending your elbow and placing the palm of the opposite hand on the tip of the elbow. Then place the thumb on the very end of the elbow crease and press directly in toward the bone. Large Intestine 11 can often relieve itching anywhere in the body. It can also relieve tendinitis and bursitis. If used with Large Intestine 4, the healing power is enhanced and quickened.

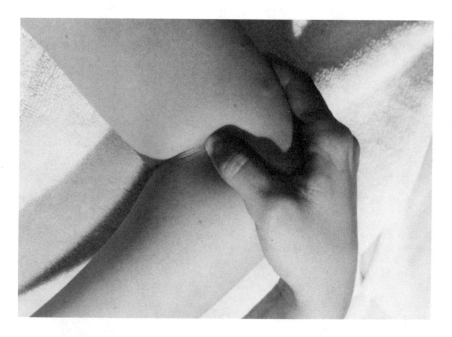

Figure 5. Large Intestine 11.

4. Stomach 36

Stomach 36 is about four inches below the knee along the outside edge of the tibia (the large bone). To locate Stomach 36, place the ball of your hand on the knee cap and stretch your fingers out without moving the hand. Let your middle finger touch the outside edge of the tibia bone. The tip of your middle finger will be on Stomach 36.

Stomach 36 has a nick name the "wake-em up point," because

the stomach channel goes from the middle of the lower socket of the eye straight down the front of the body down to your toes. Stimulating Stomach 36 will send qi to your eyes. I call it the lower torso power point because it can be used for many things. These include abdominal upset, stomach aches and cramps, symptoms of pre-menstrual syndrome, irregular menstruation, knee pain, ankle

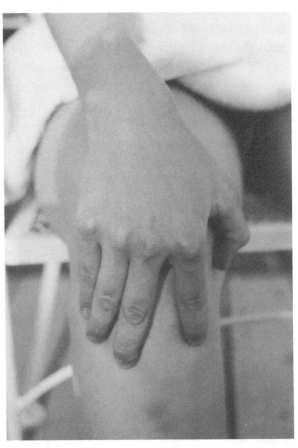

Figure 6. Stomach 36.

pain, and generally opening up qi and blood circulation to the entire body. On a general basis, problems of qi blockage from the chest down to the toes can be helped with this point.

5. Spleen 6

The next point is Spleen 6, located four inches above the inner ankle on the back edge of the tibia. This point may be especially tender because it is the only point in the entire body where three energy channels converge...the Spleen, Kidney, and Liver channels.

The health of muscles is dependent on Spleen qi. The health of the tendons is dependent upon Liver qi, and the bones are dependent upon Kidney qi. Stimulation of Spleen 6 can help people involved in sports to better reach peak performance. It can also reduce the recovery time for injuries and strengthen muscles. Spleen 6 is also useful in the treatment of impotency. In humor we say it takes three women to treat impotency. The Spleen, Liver, and Kidney are solid organs and that makes them Yin and female, hence the jest.

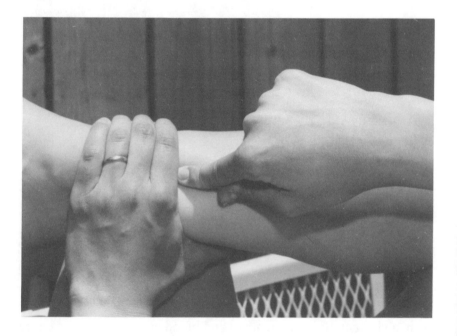

Figure 7. Spleen 6 is located on the inner side of the tibia (large bone of the calf) four fingers width above the ankle bone.

6. Kidney 1

Kidney 1 is on the bottom of the foot in the indentation that forms in the ball of your foot when you flex your toes down when barefoot. Stimulation of Kidney 1 is helpful in energizing the entire body and, when pressed hard, can influence circulation of the heart.

In TCM theory, Kidney is the mother of Heart. Therefore, when you stimulate the mother, you energize the son. Mother/son relationships are described in charts of the Five Elements.

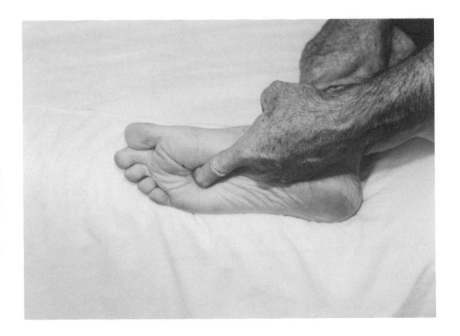

Figure 8. Kidney 1.

7. Ear Points

Another area people can learn to use is the ear. The ear energy points represent every part and function of the body. The body map of these points resembles a fetus in utero, with the lobe of the ear being the head. Therefore, if you are having a pain in one part of the body, you might be able to obtain relief by massaging the corresponding area of the ear. You can rub one or both of your ears. However, according to theories of TCM, you usually need to rub the ear on the opposite side of the pain. This theory is called the Law of the Opposites.

Other similar "body maps" can be found in the hand and on the bottom of the foot.

Chapter 7: THE QIGONG EXERCISES

"Inhaling and exhaling helps to rid one of the stale and take in the fresh. Moving as a bear and stretching as a bird can result in longevity."

Ancient Chinese Saying

"Flow with whatever may happen and let your mind be free.
Stay centered by accepting whatever you are doing. This is the ultimate."

Chuang Tzu

This chapter describes Qigong exercises presented by Dr. Chow:

The Qigong exercises described below are part of "The Chow Integrated Healing System" to awaken the qi within you quickly, yet carefully. In my experience of over thirty-five years, I find it is unwise for people in the West to practice Qigong exercises without also practicing the philosophies and supportive measures described in Chapters 5 and 6. This is because Westerners with a more complex life style are more likely to have serious and different energy imbalances and blockages than people living in China. These energy disturbances can be amplified with Qigong practice, and this may lead to side effects.

Even in China, Qigong and other methods of TCM are not practiced as isolated therapies. For example, people seldom go to a doctor of TCM and receive a treatment with only acupuncture or only herbs, common events in the West. Practitioners of TCM evaluate their patients in a thorough manner. They begin by diagnosing the type of energy disturbance present, then recommend a program of therapies that may include meditation, acupuncture, herbs, diet, massage, and Qigong, as well as other treatments. I carry out a similar type of practice.

One of the secrets of my success is the application of a program consisting of a mixture of philosophies and health-supporting measures. If you want to receive the maximum benefit from Qigong, you need to do likewise. This helps to establish normal balance and harmony in the body, mind, and spirit: this is the basis of activating our built-in healing responses.

As you practice these exercises you will become more sensitive to the qi. You may not notice anything at first. Persist, have patience, practice daily, and you may be rewarded with a quantum leap in your development.

Exercises presented in this chapter should not be confused with ordinary calisthenics, which they are not. This set of exercises has been modified from Qigong maneuvers that have been in use for centuries. An instructional videotape is available.

FITTING THESE EXERCISES INTO YOUR SCHEDULE

Early morning is the best time for Qigong practice, during what is referred to in TCM theory as the "rising Yang in the Yin energy." Everything has been at rest during the night and the air is more likely to be clean and pure. Early morning practice helps regulate the mind and body to cope with stresses during the day and increases efficiency. Therefore, it is advised that you develop a pattern of exercising for thirty minutes in the morning, and another thirty minutes during the evening or before bedtime. If you become fatigued during the afternoon, you can do a few exercises at that time as well.

A unique aspect of these exercises is that they stimulate the body in the morning, yet promote sleep when done before bedtime. The same exercises produce tonification (stimulation) or sedation according to what the body needs at the time.

It also is advised that you meditate for twenty minutes in the morning and another twenty minutes in the evening. This involves a total commitment of fifty minutes, twice a day. These times can be shortened but results will be related directly to the time invested.

After practicing diligently for about six months, most people become sensitive enough to feel their qi and can determine how much time they need to devote to practice each day to maintain a good energy level. When that point is reached, the time needed for practice can be individualized. Generally it can be reduced.

The exercises are numbered from #1 to #17. Exercises #1 through #4 are basic, require only a little spare time, and can be done anywhere, anytime. Exercise #5, "Standing at the Stake," is handled differently. I suggest that while you are learning these exercises, you spend some extra time on this one. Gradually build up the time you are able to do Standing at the Stake. Try to increase your time until you can do it for one full hour. If you can't increase the time, that's all right. After you have found that you can perform this exercise well, about ten minutes per day is adequate.

Each exercise from #6 through #17 requires a minimum amount of time to be completed adequately. Don't rush the exercises simply because you feel like squeezing all of them into the time you have allocated for practice. If you hurry these exercises, you will not find them to be as effective. As with all exercises, if you overexert, you may injure yourself.

You begin activating qi by rubbing your laogong points together. Then proceed by doing Standing at the Stake for ten minutes. Then do the warm-up exercises (#6 through #9). Follow with the Precious Eight exercises (#10 through #17). Always do the exercises in the order presented: they have been designed in a specific sequence according to energy theories of TCM.

When your allocated time comes to an end, simply stop where you are and make a note of the last exercise completed. In the ensuing practice session, start with the next exercise in the sequence. When you have completed exercise #17, begin again with #5. Continue this rotation through all of your exercises. The amount of time you want to devote to Qigong will depend upon your goals.

People who are trying to recover from an illness should complete several sets of the exercises at least three times per day. People who are seriously ill should practice these measures almost on a full time basis.

Remember to have patience and you will get quicker results. Do the exercises with regularity. Practice the exercises with another person or in a group if possible: this assists in the motivation of the qi and usually helps to activate the qi more powerfully.

I wish you good luck.

EXPERIENCES FROM DOING THE EXERCISES

People observe different effects from practicing the exercises:
1) Some immediately notice changes or sensations in the body. Sometimes very subtle changes are the most important as they may signify greater long term change.
2) Others have delayed effects, while still others have no obvious changes or sensations. Don't be disappointed by this. Even if you feel nothing, something is happening to the energy in your body.
3) A present health condition may worsen before improving. Infrequently, pain may increase when an energy block is removed or released. This is generally a temporary condition. In my long experience with these exercises there have not been any reports of any serious problems.

THE PRELIMINARY EXERCISES

The following two exercises are among the most important Qigong exercises. They should become incorporated into your daily routine until they become automatic. These first two exercises help your body to absorb more oxygen and this makes the succeeding exercises more effective.

EXERCISE #1

Proper Posture: The Silver Thread.

Please refer back to pages 80-84 to review details covered on posture. Stand or sit up straight, using the spine as your support, not the back of a chair. Visualize a straight silver thread extending from the ground up through the tailbone (Governing Vessel point #1) on up the spine to the top of your head (to Governing Vessel point #20, the Point of 100 Reasons). Imagine that the silver thread extends up from the top point of your head, the "bai wei," to the heavens, and that you are being pulled upward by this thread.

Feel that this pulling action is stretching your spine. Roll your shoulders backward and down, away from your neck. Feel your back muscles and scapulae (shoulder blades) drop down. Let everything relax around the silver thread and let your head and the base of your neck become flexible. Feel that you are a willow tree instead of an oak tree. The willow is soft and bends easily, the oak does not.

This posture may feel awkward at first, but remember that a person with a good posture looks better and feels more self-confident. Most important, it allows one to breathe properly so as to get sufficient oxygen to feed and enhance the internal qi.

EXERCISE #2

Breathing with the Diaphragm

You may wish to review the details of diaphragmatic breathing that were covered on pages 80-84. As mentioned previously, we all need to relearn how to breathe properly, and to breathe with our diaphragms all the time.

When you are doing the following exercises, there is one additional step involved in how you should breathe. With the diaphragm area expanding out, inhale air through the nostrils. With the diaphragm area contracting in, let air out through the lips in a small, steady stream. During inhalation the tip of the tongue should be touching the line where the roof of the mouth (palate) meets the upper front teeth.

This position forms a connection between one energy channel (the Governing Vessel) and another (the Conception Vessel) and allows energy to flow normally between the two. When you breath out, lightly drop the tip of your tongue.

When you are breathing properly, the stream of air coming out through the lips should be so fine that it will not disturb a down feather at close range. Try to breathe in and out as deeply and slowly as possible; never force the breath. With practice you should be able to breathe in and out at a rate of four smooth breaths per minute with ease and continue this indefinitely.

Proper posture is a prerequisite for proper breathing. Anytime you feel stressed, focus on your posture, breathe with your diaphragm and relax. When properly done, these exercises have helped many people relieve long-term pain as well as other problems.

Exercises #3 and #4 are important in helping you become sensitive and feel your qi. They prepare you to use the qi to relax tensions. With further study and experience, you can use your own qi for healing.

EXERCISE #3

Activating the Qi via the Laogong Point

This exercise helps most people begin to feel qi right away, or after practicing only a short time. It is also all right if at first you don't seem to feel anything. Feeling qi takes practice. It also depends upon your sensitivity to feelings and an acknowledgement of minute impressions. How effectively you use qi depends upon the practice and skills you will learn later.

Step 1. Start by pretending that you are outside and the temperature is ten degrees below zero. Do whatever you ordinarily would do to keep warm. You might want to jump around, rub your hands, pat yourself, etc. Take note of how you feel and your level of warmth.

Step 2. Now, roll your hand into a fist. Find the point in your palm between the middle and ring fingers. This point is called the laogong (hard working) point. The laogong point also is known as Pericardium 8 because it is point number eight on the Pericardium energy channel. This energy channel flows from the heart area outward on the middle inner aspect of the arm through the palm to the thumb side of the tip of the middle finger.

Rub your palms together vigorously so that the laogong points of each palm touch as you do so. Note the level of warmth in your palms, hands, arms, face and any other part of your body. Do you feel different from how you normally would when you try to keep yourself warm, as in step 1? Do you feel more heat in your hands? Do you feel heat or other sensations in any other parts of your body? Let yourself be as sensitive as possible to, and acknowledge the slightest changes or sensations, even if they are fleeting.

EXERCISE #4

Sensing Qi

Step 1. After rubbing your laogong points together vigorously, hold your palms facing each other about one or two inches apart for about three to five minutes. Concentrate on the sensation between the palms but also be aware of feelings in your entire body. Do you feel anything such as heat, tingling, or pulsating sensations? Let your creative self acknowledge whatever you sense.

Step 2. Now move your palms apart slowly and steadily to about four inches, then back to the original position. Repeat this action many times. Take note of what you feel. Let yourself be sensitive to any sensations. Acknowledge even the slightest sensations between the palms, in your hands or in any other part of your body, without analysis or censorship. When you feel definite and strong sensations, slowly and steadily move your palms farther apart. Stop before you reach the point where you no longer feel any sensations, then move your hands closer together again. As you continue this process repeatedly, your sensitivity will increase. When you do this for the first time, do not worry if you do not feel anything.

Step 3. Identify areas of your body where you feel tension. Relax these areas by using your qi-activated palms to brush over each area in one direction only, lightly and slowly. Be aware of what you feel. This process can help relax your muscles and reduce tension. Keep practicing daily to become more proficient.

Figure 1. Bowing to give thanks to a higher power for this universal healing qi.

Practice this exercise at least three times a day for about ten minutes each time and whenever you have idle hands.

The following exercises should be practiced twice daily, in sequence, as described. Before beginning these exercises you should take a moment to bow to the Universe (Figure 1) in thanks for giving us this wonderful energy that can heal and keep us well.

EXERCISE #5

Standing at the Stake

This exercise is done standing in a horse-stance. To find the horse-stance, begin by standing in good posture with your feet together. Place your weight on your heels and rotate your toes outward until they form as straight a line across as possible. Then, put your weight on your toes and rotate your heels out so that your toes are pointed slightly in. You should end up standing with your feet about as far apart as your shoulders, slightly pigeon-toed.

Figure 2. Horse-stance, front view.

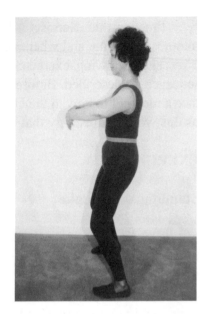

Figure 3. Horse-stance, side view.

Take note of where your feet are. In subsequent practice simply move your left foot out to this position in any exercise that requires the horse-stance which needs to be done with your feet apart. When you have established your horse-stance, come back to a feet-together stance by moving your left foot in.

In the last exercise you learned how to activate the laogong point. Now, rub your laogong points together and feel the qi between your palms. As you move this qi into the circle of your arms, move your left foot out into the horse-stance. Hold your arms at heart level with your fingers pointing towards each other about one inch apart, palms facing your torso. Relax your muscles, even though you are holding up your arms. Drop your shoulders back and relax them. Breathe slowly and rhythmically with the diaphragm. Bend your knees slightly and keep your posture straight.

This exercise helps to develop stamina and increase the dantian qi (the dantian is an energy storage area located two inches below the navel and one inch in). It also develops patience and knowledge of how to manage each part of your body. If a particular part of your body becomes tired such as your shoulders or your arms, mentally drop those muscles as you breathe out to relax them. Breathing rhythmically and smoothly, try to stand in this position as long as possible, gradually building up to one hour. Remember to do the exercise only to the point of what I call becoming "comfortably uncomfortable."

If you must stop to rest because of aching muscles, use exercise #4, step 3, to brush your sore muscles. Brushing lightly in one direction, feel the tension in your muscles gradually fade away. Then resume the "Standing At The Stake" exercise.

While doing this exercise you should concentrate on your breathing and how you feel. Don't let other thoughts enter your mind or interrupt your concentration. If thoughts come, just acknowledge them and let them leave your mind. Let them pass through and soon all thoughts will have passed. Whatever noises there may be, pleasant or unpleasant, acknowledge them and leave them in the distant background. Listen with your dantian.

In TCM the dantian is called the "seat of life" where qi, your vital energy or life force, is stored in the body. Feel a solidness at the dantian. Balance your weight on both feet. Feel the silver thread pulling you up and that you are holding the position very easily. With practice, you will feel a cushion under your arms: they might even feel weightless.

This is a very important basic exercise to master before progressing to other still or moving Qigong exercises because it demands ultimate discipline of body, mind, and spirit. You should begin to feel an energy pulsation in the fingertips and through the arms. After standing for a while, move your fingertips away, then back closer again. You should begin to feel a similar pull and resistance of energy between your fingertips just as you did in activating the laogong point and in sensing the qi in exercises #3 and #4.

In spite of an apparently inactive posture, you may feel energy moving up to the face and head and throughout the body. Some people have reported that they feel as if they have run ten miles. They feel flushed, sweaty, and have a very red facial complexion. The "Standing At The Stake" exercise is excellent for cardiovascular circulation. It demands patience and stamina. When you have mastered this exercise, you can accomplish many things. Good luck at Standing at the Stake.

Remember the following while doing all of the exercises:

1) Maintain a good posture, keeping the spine stretched.
2) Breathe in as you move into an exercise and breathe out as you move out of an exercise.
3) Move very slowly and evenly. Do not bounce, rock, or force a movement.
4) Relax the muscles in moving and stretching. Do not tighten your muscles.
5) Stretch only to the point of being "comfortably uncomfortable," not painful.
6) Progress at your own pace. Have patience and fun. Persist daily and you will gain a great deal. Take note of all changes, big or small.

WARM UP EXERCISES

We now begin the Warm-up Qigong exercises of The Chow Integrated Healing System. This set of four warm-up exercises progressively and carefully loosens up bodily structures and joints, fosters the circulation of qi in the internal organs, and encourages relaxation. It also increases the internal qi with an emphasis on concentration and discipline for the body, mind, and spirit. The exercises prepare us for action.

EXERCISE #6

The Side Stretch: Warm-up Exercise #1

This exercise loosens up and stretches the spine and side muscles from the head and neck down the entire side of the body to the feet.

Stand with good posture and breathe properly, with your feet together, knees straight, arms down at the sides and seat tucked in (Figure 6-1).

Slowly drop your head to the right side as far as you can (Figure 6-2). Then gradually arch your body over to that side. Extend the spinal silver thread and stretch your spine while you arch into the shape of a letter "C." Try to point the "bai wei" energy point (Governing Vessel point #20 at the top of the head) to the floor as much as you can (Figure 6-3).

Figure 6-1.

Figure 6-2.

Figure 6-3.

As you bend, be certain to stretch your spine. Drop and relax your muscles. Instead of tensing up, relax your body as you go into your stretch. If you relax you will be able to stretch more. When you have stretched over as far as possible with your body in a C-shaped curve, count from one to ten slowly. With each count, allow yourself to relax and bend further. Resist any tendency to bounce in order to hold the bend. Just slowly persist in relaxing. As you continue to stretch the spine, roll back upwards beginning with your waist. Your head should straighten up last. Your spine never should be in the shape of a S-shaped curve. Always keep it in a C-shaped curve to prevent an injury.

Breathe in as you move down and breathe out as you move up. Repeat this exercise to the left. Do this exercise eight times alternately to each side, counting to ten at the bottom of each bend until you reach a total count of 160.

EXERCISE #7

The Propeller Turn: Warm-up #2

This exercise increases the flexibility of the waist and hips, strengthens the arms and shoulders, tightens the abdominal muscles and develops stamina.

Assume a horse-stance. As you step into your horse-stance bring your arms, palms up, to shoulder height. Be sure that your shoulders are relaxed and dropped down away from the head as much as possible. With elbows slightly flexed, the arms should be straight out to the side at shoulder height with the head and body facing straight forward (Figure 7-1).

Keep your footing solid. Without moving your arms or head out of position, rotate your total upper body from the waist and hips to the right while you stretch the spinal column and relax your muscles (Figure 7-2).

Turn as far as possible. Bend your knees to allow for a greater rotation. Continue to turn as far as you can. Stretch the spine, relax the muscles, and turn some more (Figure 7-3).

When you've turned as far as possible, count from one to ten slowly, each time trying to turn further. Never bounce in your movement. Gently hold your turn, then try to turn some more. It is possible to turn 180 degrees around when you become more flexible.

Figure 7-1

Figure 7-2

After the count of ten, rotate back very slowly to the forward

position. Breathe in as you turn to the back and breathe out as you turn to the front again. Do this exercise eight times alternately to each side until you have reached a total count of 160.

Figure 7-3.

EXERCISE #8

The Hip Rotation: Warm-up Exercise #3

This exercise is very important and accomplishes many things. It can help:

1)   Lubricate and increase the flexibility of the hips and knee joints to prevent a common condition known as osteoporosis.
2)   Facilitate intestinal activity and circulation of the internal organs (with the potential of improving digestion, elimination, sexual energy, and function).
3)   Loosen the lower back muscles and prevent as well as assist in the healing of back pains.
4)   Strengthen the thigh, leg and ankle muscles.
5)   Achieve better flexibility in general.
6)   Tighten the abdominal muscles. Many people have lost many inches around their waist and hips from this exercise.

Standing in good posture and breathing properly with your feet together, rub the laogong point in your hands to feel the heat (Figure 8-1).

As you place the laogong point on the kidney point of your bladder meridian in the lower back, step into the horse-stance. Your gaze should be focused about thirty to forty feet in front of you. Your hands should be aligned with the fingers pointing downward and parallel to each other. Bring your elbows back toward your spine and your shoulders back relaxed in order to open your chest and lungs and take in oxygen better (Figures 8-2, 8-3, and 8-4).

Keeping your body above the waist stationary and facing straight ahead, rotate your hips in as large a circle as you can. First rotate clockwise by moving your hips to the left then forward as your hips rotate to the right, then backwards and around to the left and continue for ten cycles. Now, reverse the direction to counter-clockwise rotations. Pretend that you are standing in a pond of water and turning your hips to make as large a swirl in the water as possible. (Figures 8-5, 8-6, 8-7, 8-8, and 8-9).

Bending your knees makes the rotation easier and helps to strengthen the legs and knees. Do the rotations to the right to the count of ten, then reverse and rotate to the left to the count of ten. Inhale as you go into the rotation and exhale as you come out, so that with each circular movement there is one complete breath.

Keep your alignment straight over the center line between your feet. Do not move your upper body from side to side: only your hips should move. Try to feel the bending and flexing of your waist and feel the organs moving inside the abdomen. Imagine that qi, blood, and gastric juices are flowing very well. Repeat these hip rotations ten times to each side alternately until you have reached the total count of 160. When you have finished, step back into position with your feet together, bring your hands back down to your sides and stand in good posture. Feel what your body has just experienced.

Figure 8-1.

Figure 8-2

Figure 8-3, Side View.

Figure 8-4, Back View.

Figure 8-5.

Figure 8-6.

Figure 8-7.

Figure 8-8.

Figure 8-9, Side View.

EXERCISE #9

The Knee Rotation: Warm-up Exercise #4

This exercise increases the flexibility of the knees, ankles and hips. It helps to strengthen the thigh and leg muscles. By making the knees and ankles more flexible, this exercise also helps reduce the risk of knee and ankle injuries. Some people, even noted ballet dancers, joggers, and other sports enthusiasts, do not have lateral movement of their knees. Often they can't rotate their knees and can only make up and down and straight forward movements. Developing lateral movement helps to make you more flexible so that if you trip or lose your balance, you have less risk for injury. This is also a very good exercise for people who have knee and ankle pain or weakness of muscles in the legs.

Stand in good posture with your feet together, knees straight, breathe properly and rub your laogong points together. Place your hands over your knee caps. Bend over with your head up, shoulders relaxed and down, the back straight, and your eyes looking about thirty to forty feet straight ahead (Figure 9-1).

Now, slowly move your knees to the left (Figure 9-2) and then rotate them downward as far as they can bend without lifting your heels off of the ground (Figures 9-3 and 9-4). This helps to stretch the Achilles tendon at the back of the heel.

Then rotate your knees to the right (Figure 9-5) and come back up straight. Continue in a smooth flow to the next rotation. Use your hands to help push your knees through these movements.

Your body should be kept in a straight alignment. Do not swing your hips around because this would reduce the movement of the knees. This exercise is similar to slalom skiing in which the knees move from side to side but the body stays pointed straight down the hill. With each circular rotation, complete one breath in and out. When you finish your rotations, bring yourself up slowly to a proper standing position. Breathe deeply and notice how the exercise makes you feel. Gradually, you will be able to rotate your knees in a wider and wider circle and you will be able to bend down more, stretching the Achilles tendon.

Figure 9-1.

Do the rotations ten times to the left, then ten times to the right. Continue until you have reached a total count of 160.

Remember to do these exercises to the point of being comfortably uncomfortable. Stop to rest if you must before you begin again. To encourage relaxation and control when resting, brush the energy lightly down your hips and legs in one direction.

Figure 9-2

Figure 9-3

Figure 9-4.

Figure 9-5.

THE CHOW "PRECIOUS EIGHT EXERCISES"

We now begin the Chow "Precious Eight" Qigong exercises. This set of Precious Eight exercises progressively and carefully loosens up bodily structures and joints. The exercises foster the development of internal qi with an emphasis on concentration and discipline for the body, mind, and spirit. They prepare us for action and lead us into movement.

Remember the following in doing any of these exercises: If you have some kind of physical problem or physical disability that prevents you from performing a full exercise, do as much of the exercise as you can. People who are wheelchair bound have benefitted from doing these exercises even though they could not stand up on their feet. People who are bedridden can still go through the arm, leg, and head movements shown. Do as much of each exercise as you can, as well as you can.

EXERCISE #10

Heavenly Stretch: Precious Eight Qigong Exercise #1

This exercise will help stretch the body muscles and structure lengthwise, tighten the abdominal muscles, loosen the shoulder muscles and tendons, and reduce muscle tension and spasms in the shoulders and scapula area. It is also good for improving lower back pains and promotes a general increase in qi, making it flow upward. Asthma and allergy conditions have been helped significantly. It also helps get rid of fat on the shoulders, back, and arms, and tightens muscles. For example, underarm flab usually develops toward mid-life: this exercise helps tighten the underarm muscles. It gives you a very good sense of well-being. Most people like this exercise very much.

Stand with your feet together in a proper straight posture and breathe with the diaphragm (Figure 10-1).

Look straight ahead and turn your palms outward. This will

rotate your shoulders backwards to further straighten your posture. Imagine that a silver thread extends through your arms and out through the middle fingers. Stretch your arms as much as you can without tightening your muscles.

Raise your arms slowly, stretching at the same time (Figures 10-2 and 10-3).

Keep your shoulders in place as you move your arms slowly over your head. Place your palms together (Figure 10-4).

Link your fingers together firmly as shown (Figure 10-5).

Turn your hands over so that the palms are facing the ceiling or sky (Figure 10-6).

Stretch your arms and your total body as much as you can. Then try to raise your shoulders up to your ears. This may be difficult in the beginning. You may feel stiff, but gradually you will get looser. With your elbows straightened, stretch your arms up over your head. Feel the stretch all the way down your body as far as you can, right down to your legs, calves and heels. Keep breathing in air. This stretch forces you to take more oxygen into the lungs. You can feel the flush rise up to your face.

Figure 10-1.

Figure 10-2

When you have stretched up as far as you can, slowly rise up on your toes and stretch more. Raise your shoulders up some more and feel all of your body muscles stretching. Stay up on your tip-toes. After you have stretched up as much as you can, keep your arms and elbows straight and bring your shoulders downward. Feel your entire chest wall move down and the scapula loosening up.

When you have lowered your shoulders as much as possible, unlink your fingers and push with the base of your palms out and downward to the side. Keep lowering your shoulders as you lower your arms. Start breathing out through the lips when you begin to push out and down with the base of your palms. Try to bend your wrists at a ninety degree angle with the fingers pointing straight up to heaven. You may feel qi to your fingers as a tingling sensation and warmth.

Keep lowering your arms slowly to the side and keep pushing the base of your palm out all of the way down. When your arms are at shoulder height, begin to bring your heels down as your arms come down (Figure 10-7).

Continue to bring your arms down with the wrists bent at ninety degree angles. These movements should be deliberate to the final point of relaxing your fingers completely (Figure 10-8).

Do this exercise with one complete breath. Breathe in as you raise your arms up and breathe out as you lower your arms. If you need to take another breath because you are running out of breath, then do so. However, know that you have cheated and attempt to control your breath longer each time you do this exercise. Do not lower your arms faster just because you are running out of breath. Discipline yourself and continue to work at this until you are able to complete these arm movements with one slow breath. Repeat this exercise eight times in each session.

Figure 10-3.

Figure 10-4.

Figure 10-5.

Figure 10-6.

Figure 10-7.   Figure 10-8.

EXERCISE #11

The Bow and Arrow: Precious Eight Qigong Exercise #2

This exercise stretches your arm and body muscles, your shoulder and chest muscles, and expands your chest wall. It teaches you to manage your shoulder and neck muscles, tone up arm muscles, and helps your head make more flexible turns. The horse-stance helps to strengthen your legs. This is also a very good exercise for people who have respiratory problems.

Stand in a proper posture with your feet together. Briskly rub the laogong points together. As you step into your horse-stance raise both of your hands up with your palms facing your chin. The left palm should be closer to your face and the right palm should be behind the left. Always leave about an inch of space between the palms. That allows a cushion of qi to build up. That is your starting position (Figure 11-1).

Now, you can move your arms into the bow and arrow position...to the right first. Slowly open your arms to the side at shoulder level (Figure 11-2, 11-3, and 11-4).

Keep the rest of the body still. Extend your right arm to your side at shoulder height. With the forefinger pointing up to heaven, try to bend your wrist as close to a ninety degree angle as possible with the thumb holding the other fingers into a fist. The palm should be facing outward. The other arm is bent at shoulder level with your left fist at the underarm. Your head rotates to the right to look over the right shoulder. Stretch both arms out in a straight alignment with your shoulder.

Feel the stretch in your chest, upper back and arms. Keep your abdomen flat. Breathe in as you move your arms out and breathe out as you bring your palms and your arms together again. Now, slowly move your arms back into the starting position with the palms in front of your chin and mouth. At the same time turn your head to face forward.

Pause a relaxing second, then repeat the movement to the left. This time, point with the left forefinger and turn your head to the left. When stretching outward try to feel the pull in the center line, front and back. Visualize a silver thread passing through both of your arms and someone pulling the silver thread from each side. Feel the stretch, feel the pull of the center line, front and back. This also forces you to breathe more. Review your horse-stance from Exercise #5. Do this exercise alternately to each side eight times.

Figure 11-1.

Figure 11-2.

Figure 11-3.

Figure 11-4.

EXERCISE #12

Heaven and Earth Stretch: Precious Eight Qigong Exercise #3

This exercise stretches the torso muscles diagonally as well as stretching the muscles of the arms. Begin with the feet together. As in the previous exercise, raise palms up to face the chin. The left hand should be inside of the right. In this exercise, both arms should move in unison (Figure 12-1).

Gradually rotate the palm of the left hand upward toward heaven and the palm of the right hand down toward the earth (Figure 12-2). Slowly raise your left hand and lower your right. Keep both hands in the midline as long as possible (Figure 12-3). Continue to raise the left hand until it is straight over the head. Bend the left wrist ninety degrees so the palm faces heaven. Simultaneously lower the right arm straight down until it is at the side of the body. Bend the right wrist to form a ninety degree angle. The palm of the right hand should face the earth. The fingers of both hands should face to the right. As your arms move slowly, rotate your head ninety degrees to the right (Figure 12-4). Now stretch your torso muscles diagonally by pushing with your palms and stretching your arms. Keep your posture straight. Do not bend over or tilt your head. Stretch as much as you can to the point of being "comfortably uncomfortable." Slowly move both arms back to the original position with palms facing the chin-mouth area. At the same time slowly rotate your head forward, synchronizing with the movement of your arms. Now, reverse sides and turn your right hand up toward heaven, moving your arm straight up. Imagine you are pushing heaven up. The right hand is bent at a right angle at the wrist and your fingers should point to the left. At the same time, turn your left palm downward along the center line of the body moving toward the side. With the palm at right angles, push the palm toward the floor. Both hands and fingers should point to the left. As you move your arms, rotate your head slowly to the left. Repeat this exercise eight times to each side alternately. Remember to keep the body straight as you stretch the muscles diagonally.

Figure 12-1

Figure 12-2

Figure 12-3.

Figure 12-4.

EXERCISE #13

Head and Eyes Rotation: Precious Eight Qigong Exercise #4

This exercise will help you manage the neck muscles and prevent them from stiffening or tightening up. It helps to relieve headaches and pains in the neck, shoulders, arms and back. It increases the range of motion of the head and neck. For example, when we drive a car we often must turn and look behind to check for traffic. Many people are not able to turn only their head far enough to see the "blind" spot, but must turn their entire body. This exercise can enable people to turn their heads and see behind them without needing to turn the entire body.

The neck area is a key problem area that can cause pain in any part of the body, including the feet and hands. It is extremely important to know how to relax these neck and shoulder muscles and the occiput area (the lower back of the head). You need to have full command of these muscles to relax and stretch them so they will stay loose and relaxed. Very important...this exercise also helps to increase the field of vision and frequently helps to improve the eyesight.

Figure 13-1.

Stand with your feet together in proper straight Silver Thread posture and breathe with the diaphragm. Look straight ahead. Without turning or moving any other part of your body, rotate your head slowly to the right (Figure 13-1).

When you have rotated your head as far as you can, look to the right as far as possible at eye level without over-straining. Notice how far you can turn your head and eyes (Figure 13-2).

Then, with your mind and thought (as well as physically), stretch that silver thread and your spine up as far as it will go. At the same time drop all of your muscles and turn your head some more. Try to see further to the right (Figure 13-3).

Figure 13-2.   Figure 13-3.

You will find that you will be able to turn your head a little more and can see further around. Hold your head there, then stretch up, turn your head again a second time and look even further. Hold your head there, again stretch up and turn your head a third time and look further.

Each time you probably will be able to turn your head a little more and see further around the other side of your body. Try to see the opposite shoulder! Take note of how much more flexible you are. Now, slowly turn your head and eyes forward to the original position.

Reverse the direction and do these exercises to the left, carrying out the same actions.

Repeat this exercise eight times to each side alternately. Remember to keep your body straight. You will be surprised at how far you can turn your head and how much further you can see around the back of you!

EXERCISE #14

The Upper Torso Rotation: Precious Eight Qigong Exercise #5

This exercise helps to loosen all of the joints and muscles in the body. Care must be taken to do this gently to avoid over-exertion. Don't force any movement. Drop and relax your upper torso as it rotates around. Arch over only as far you can comfortably. You will improve with practice.

Start by assuming the horse-stance. Place your hands on your upper thigh hip joints with fingers facing forward and your thumbs facing backward to the sides. Then, while maintaining good posture, bend your knees (Figure 14-1).

Turn your head to face left and roll your torso forward, dropping your head first. Roll down as far as you can with your knees bent (Figures 14-2, 14-3, and 14-4).

Slowly move your hips to the left. Drop your shoulders, arms, upper body, and head, letting them fall in the opposite direction of your hips. Keep your body in a C-shaped arch (Figure 14-5).

Continue rotating your hips to the front as your upper body drops backward, dropping your shoulders and elbows back (Figures 14-6, 14-7, 14-8, and 14-9).

The key is to relax all of your muscles and joints in your rotation and not force them. Then, move your hips to the right and drop your upper body, head, and shoulders to the left (Figure 14-10, 14-11, and 14-12).

Continue to rotate your hips to the back and drop your upper body, head, and shoulders down to the front until you are bent over fully from the waist with your head down (Figure 14-13 and 14-14).

Then roll your torso up first from the hips keeping your head dropped down until you are straight up and in an upright standing position to the finishing position. This prevents possibly throwing your back out and causing strain or pain (Figures 14-15 and 14-16).

With each rotation breathe in and out once. Breathe in going into the rotation, breathe out coming out of the rotation. Remember to drop your head first, as part of a downward motion of your torso, and to bring your head up last, as part of the upward motion of your torso.

Now, do the exercise in the reverse direction. Do this exercise to each side alternately eight times. It is always best to do this exercise in sequence with the other Precious Eight Qigong exercises because you need to limber up your body before attempting to do each subsequent exercise.

Figure 14-1.

Figure 14-2.

Figure 14-3.

Figure 14-4.

Figure 14-5.

Figure 14-6.

Figure 14-7.

Figure 14-8.

Figure 14-9.

Figure 14-10.

Figure 14-11.

Figure 14-12.

Figure 14-13.

Figure 14-14.

Figure 14-15.   Figure 14-16.

EXERCISE #15

Back Arm Raise: Precious Eight Qigong Exercise #6

This exercise opens up the lung and chest cavity which improves breathing. It stretches and relaxes the shoulder and back muscles and improves the rotation of the shoulder joints. It also improves balance.

Because this exercise opens up the heart and chest, it makes a person extremely vulnerable. All of the other exercises have brought the student up to the point of being able to say, "It's all right. I am vulnerable and I am able to face anything."

Stand in proper good posture with your feet together. Link your fingers together behind you with the palms facing upward. Straighten your arms and turn your elbows inward toward the spine. Pull your shoulders up and backward so the muscles over the collarbone and the chest wall will stretch (Figure 15-1, 15-2, 15-3).

Keep your head and posture straight at all times throughout this exercise. Do not stick your head out or curve your body. Now, begin to raise your arms out and upward. If you need to, have a friend help you by supporting your hands or wrists as you move your arms in an outward and upward arch (Figure 15-4).

As your arms move upward, balance on your toes. Continue to pull your shoulders back and raise your hands up as far as you can (Figure 15-5).

Do not roll the shoulder joints forward. If you are beginning to bend over, do not raise your arms any higher. The key is to be able to maintain a straight posture and elevate the arms as high as possible. With practice, some people can raise their arms up to the level of their shoulders. Others, who are especially flexible, can raise their arms even higher! Do this exercise at your own capability and speed and do not overstrain. Gradually your flexibility will improve.

Breathe in as you raise your arms and balance on your toes. Breathe out as you bring your arms down and lower your heels to the ground very slowly.

After reaching up as high as you can, bring the shoulders backward as far as possible without over-straining. Then come down with your arms synchronizing with the lowering of your heels.

Do the exercise eight times. Each time you elevate your arms hold them there and try to relax while holding that position.

Figure 15-1.

Figure 15-2, Side View.

Figure 15-3, Back View.

Figure 15-4.

Figure 15-5.

EXERCISE #16

The Punch: Precious Eight Qigong Exercise #7

Figure 16-1.

The previous exercise (#15) brings you to the point of being vulnerable and open to the Universe. This exercise provides a defensive, protective mechanism for the individual. Stand with a horse-stance. Form fists with your hands and hold them at the sides of your waist with the elbows bent back toward the spine. Hold the shoulders back in a good posture and bend the knees. Keep your body and head completely still. Move only your arms. The fingers of your fists should be turned upward (Figure 16-1). Concentrate your attention about thirty to forty feet ahead. As you begin to move your arm forward, turn the fist over so it faces the ground as it passes the level of the diaphragm (Figure 16-2 and 16-3). Then strike forward with a full extension of the arm with the fist ending up at chin level (Figure 16-4, 16-5). Don't thrust your shoulders forward. Don't move any other part of the body except the arms. Then bring the fist back, turning it at the level of the diaphragm so that the fingers of the fist face upward when it is at the side of the waist. Then return the arms to the beginning position with the fists facing up. Do this exercise eight times alternatively, starting with the right. You can think of frustrations you want to let go of when doing this exercise. Inhale as you strike out, exhale as you bring your fist back to the waist. When you have completed the exercise, step back into proper posture position with arms relaxed by the sides of the body.

Figure 16-2.

Figure 16-3.

Figure 16-4.

Figure 16-5, Side View.

EXERCISE #17

Total Body Stretch with External Qi: Precious Eight Qigong Exercise #8

In all the preceding exercises you have stretched yourself in different directions and lubricated the joints in your body, opened yourself to the Universe and learned a defensive, protective mechanism, such as the last exercise (#16). Now you are ready to experience the external qi through the laogong point. This exercise will also stretch the total body.

This exercise will stretch your body even further. It helps you to become more agile and flexible. Gradually, as you practice, you will find that you will be able to bend further and reach further at every point. This means you are managing your muscles better.

Standing with your feet together, in good posture and breathing properly, slowly raise both of your arms in front of you until they are up vertically over your head (Figures 17-1, 17-2, 17-3). As you do this, your hands should be facing each other about ten to twelve inches apart so that the laogong points can emit qi between the palms. Stretch your entire body up when your hands are straight up above your head. Do not go up on your toes in this exercise: stretch up. Raise your shoulders to your ear level and feel the stretch all the way down to your heels. Now, roll down forward dropping your head first. Roll down bringing the arms down almost straight in front of you with the laogong points still facing each other at the distance of ten to twelve inches.

Roll down as far as you can, touching your knees with your hands on the way down (Figure 17-4). Then reach with your hands and your fingers to try to touch the floor behind your feet as far as you can. Just relax and drop your torso in order to reach further (Figure 17-5).

Don't try to tighten your muscles and stretch. Just relax your muscles and your spine and you will be able to reach further. Try to touch the floor behind your feet, then try to hold the back of your legs wherever you can reach (Figure 17-6).

The ankle or the calf area may be as far as some people can reach. Pull your body down further close to your legs, bending over and relaxing your back muscles in order to bend more. Ease your elbows outward as you pull your body forward.

Now, reach with your hands and fingers to touch the floor in front of your feet. If your fingers touch the floor and you can bend further, rotate your palms upward with the fingers toward each other and see if you can touch the floor with the back of your hands. Don't tighten as you stretch. Just relax as you stretch and drop. Keep your knees straight all the time (Figure 17-7).

Relax your hands and just let your whole body drop over. Feel your body hanging from the waist and your head dropping as low as it can. Now slowly roll up from the waist, keeping your head down as long as possible (Figures 17-8 and 17-9).

When you have straightened up your body, bring your head up with your chin tucked in. Place the laogong point of the palms on the Bladder Channel on the back waist area (located at the upper crest of your pelvic bone about two inches from the spine) on each side. Place your hands there until they support your body (Figure 17-10).

Slowly arch your body backwards by bending your knees first as low as they can go (Figure 17-11).

Drop your head backward. Then arch your body back using your hands as a support on the back waist area (Figure 17-12).

If you want to arch further back, relax your muscles and arch slowly backward more by bending your knees further for more flexibility. See if you can see the floor behind you, but don't overstretch. Just do what you can to the point of being comfortably uncomfortable (Figure 17-13). Then, roll back up slowly, starting by slowly straightening your knees. Be sure to do all this very gently. Then, roll up from the hips and the waist, keeping your head dropped backwards until you come up to the straightened position. As you come up, drop your shoulders down, then raise your head up into the straight position. Relax your arms by your side as you end up in proper posture. Do this exercise eight times.

Figure 17-1.

Figure 17-2.

Figure 17-3.

Figure 17-4.

Figure 17-5.

Figure 17-6.

Figure 17-7.

Figure 17-8.

Figure 17-9.

Figure 17-10

Figure 17-11.

Figure 17-12.

Figure 17-13

This ends the Warm-up and Precious Eight Exercises. You will find that if you are diligent at trying to reach the ultimate count recommended for each exercise, your body will experience a tremendous transition from inflexibility to flexibility, from lack of energy to a surplus of energy. You also will have a feeling of well-being and strong vitality. You may even notice that the conditions from which you are suffering may be relieved totally.

Each exercise session should be concluded by bowing and giving thanks to a higher power for giving us this universal healing energy.

Chapter 8: RESEARCH IN QIGONG

"It is not Qigong that is unscientific, but that science does not yet know Qigong."

Qian Xue Sen
Chinese Scientist

Throughout history the Chinese used Qigong and TCM methods because they observed that they worked. When modern scientific methods of evaluating treatment modalities appeared during this century, the Chinese showed little interest in studying TCM methods. This attitude began to change in the 1950s, and by the early 1980s truly high quality studies began to appear.

Many Western scientific communities may have a hard time accepting Qigong for several reasons. One is a general skepticism of any work done overseas (the N.I.H. syndrome--standing for "Not Invented Here"). Another is the lack of quality of many of the studies according to a Western biomedical model. Probably the biggest problem of acceptance is that some of the results sound impossible and violate currently held concepts in physics and medicine.

The First World Conference for Academic Exchange of Medical Qigong was held in Beijing in 1988. The meeting was attended by about 600 people from China, Japan, Taiwan, Hong Kong, Australia, West Germany, Canada, and the United States. Of 137 papers presented, only three were from the United States, and one was from Canada. Almost all papers presenting hard data on Qigong originated from China. A wide range of experiments and clinical trials were presented. Brief summaries of papers are presented here to document some of the research done. Articles are numbered as in the abstracts. Complete volumes of these abstracts are available from the Qigong Institute/East West Academy of Healing Arts.

ABSTRACTS OF SELECTED PAPERS PRESENTED AT THE FIRST WORLD CONFERENCE FOR ACADEMIC EXCHANGE OF MEDICAL QIGONG, CHINA, 1988

1. A Study of the Effect of the Emitted Qi of Qigong on Human Carcinoma (cancer) Cells.

Stomach cancer cells in tissue culture were treated with emitted qi for one hour. An average of 25% of qi-treated cancer cells died or were inactivated. In control samples all cancer cells survived. This study was repeated 41 times with similar results.

In a parallel study cancer cells from the uterine cervix were treated with emitted qi for 20 minutes. 31% of cancer cells were either killed or inactivated. In control samples all cancer cells survived. This study was repeated 20 times and the killing and inactivation rates ranged between 13 and 36%. (Feng Li-da, and Qian Ju Qing, China Immunology Research Center, Beijing, China)

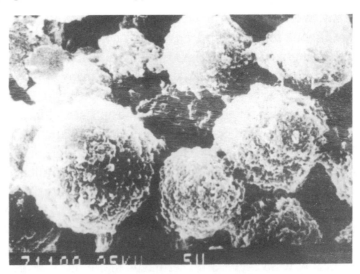

Figure 1. Stomach cancer cells from a tissue culture, magnified 3,200 times by an electronmicroscope. Note the cells have rough surfaces.

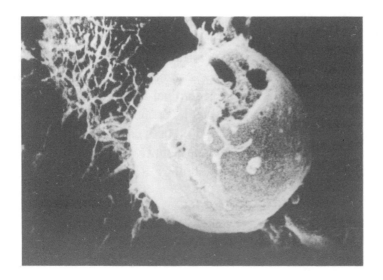

Figure 2. A stomach cancer cell that was treated with emitted qi for one hour. The surface is no longer rough and pores (holes) indicate the cell is about to disintegrate. Photos courtesy of Feng Li-da, M.D., Ph.D., and Qian Ju Qing.

Figure 3. Feng Li-da, M.D., Ph.D., presenting a paper at a meeting on Qigong.

2. The Effect of the Emitted Qi on the Immune Functions of Mice.

Phagocytic activity of peritoneal macrophages increased in the mice treated with emitted qi as compared to controls. Peritoneal macrophages are cells in the abdominal cavity that defend against invading organisms. They surround, consume, and destroy bacteria, viruses, and foreign material in a process called phagocytosis. The study implies that a general immune defense response was stimulated. (Feng Li-da et. al, China Immunology Research Center, Beijing, China)

3. A Study of the Effect of Emitted Qi on the L-1210 Cells of Leukemia in Mice.

It was found that leukemia (cancer) cells could be inhibited or killed with emitted qi, compared to cells in control samples. (Feng Li-da, et al, China Immunology Research Center, Beijing, China)

8. A Study of the Effects of the Emitted Qi and Healing of Experimental Bone Fractures.

The radius bone (forearm) was fractured in sixteen healthy male rabbits after they were anesthetized with intravenous pentothal. The animals were randomly divided into two groups, one of which received treatment with emitted qi. The rabbits were euthanized at two day intervals and fracture sites were examined by several means. Healing was greatly accelerated in rabbits treated with emitted qi compared with control animals that received no treatments. (Jia Lin, et al, National Research Institute of Sports Science, Beijing, China)

10. Psychological Effects of Qigong.

Thirty-five subjects practiced Qigong. A standard psychological test was administered before and after Qigong practice. Mental performance improved after practicing Qigong. Areas of improvement were memory, attention span, and thinking process. Major improvements were also seen in the stability of emotions, mood, the ability of self control, temper, will power, and speed of action. (Wang Jisheng, Institute of Psychology, Academia Sinica, Beijing, China)

15. Effects of The Emitted Qi on the Immune Function in Animals.

Animal studies showed that emitted qi could increase the white blood count, humoral immunity, cellular immunity, and non-specific immunity. In one study, animals were treated with cortisone to suppress their immune systems. After tests documented that their immune systems had been suppressed, the animals were divided into 3 groups.

One group was treated with emitted qi, and cellular immune functions returned to normal in twenty-four hours. A second group drank water that had been treated by emitted qi (called information water) and its immune function tests also returned to normal within twenty-four hours. The third group was untreated (control) and showed no improvement. (Li Caixi, et al, Xiyuan Hospital, China Academy of Traditional Chinese Medicine, Beijing, China)

35. Antitumor Meiosis Activity of the Emitted Qi in Tumor-Bearing Mice.

Melanoma (cancer) cells were injected into the tail veins of mice. Half of the animals were then treated with emitted qi. Lungs were examined for melanoma metastasis. Growth of melanoma mitoses (cancer spread) was markedly reduced in the group treated with emitted qi. (Cao Xuetao, et al, Dept. of Microbiology and Immunology and Shanghai Hospital, Second Military Medical College, Shanghai, China)

38. An Experimental Research on the Relationship Between Qigong and Choleresis.

At the conclusion of surgery to remove the gall bladder, 5 people had "T-tubes" placed in their bile ducts so bile would flow to the outside of the body. Patients practiced Qigong and served as their own controls. After Qigong practice, bile flow increased between 2.5 to 3.8 times over the flow rate at a resting state. More experienced Qigong practitioners produced more bile. (Wang Jia Lin, Yunnan Anthropotomy Research Institute, Yunnan Province, China)

43. A Study of Biological Effects of The Emitted Qi with Tradescantic Paludosa Micronuclear Technique.

Abnormalities in plants were shown to be prevented or increased according to the intent of the Qigong master. (Sun Silu, et al, Weifang Medical College, Shandong Province, China)

53. A Primary Study of the Inducing Function of the Emitted Qi of Qigong on the Biological Composition of Alpha-amylose in Wheat Seeds.

Emitted qi affected the alpha amylose activity of wheat seeds. Several previous studies have shown that emitted qi can raise the budding rate of rice seeds. (Liu Haitao, et al, Weifang Medical College, Shandong Province, China)

59. A Research Study on the "Anti-Aging" Effect of Qigong.

A group of 204 patients with high blood pressure were randomly divided into two groups. The control group took small doses of high blood pressure medicine, but did not practice Qigong. The study group took low doses of high blood pressure medicine, and also practiced Qigong. The groups were followed for twenty years. Qigong practitioners maintained better control of their blood pressures and experienced substantially lower overall death rates and stroke death rates than control patients who did not practice Qigong. (Wang Chongxing, et al, Shanghai Institute of Hypertension, Shanghai, China)

62. A Study of Treatment of Sensorineural Hearing Loss by Qigong.

Patients with hearing problems were treated. All had failed to respond to either Western medical methods or TCM methods. Fifty-four percent of patients with tinnitus (ringing in the ears) improved. In patients with hearing loss, 24% regained the ability to hear. (Zhu Jiru, et al, ENT Hospital, Shanghai Medicine University, Shanghai Qigong Association, Shanghai, China)

64. A Study of the Effect of the Emitted Qi Combined with Self-Practice of Qigong in Treating Paralysis.

43 patients with paralysis were studied. Before the study, 37 patients needed assistance in walking. After treatment, only 23 needed help in walking. After treatment, some patients previously using wheelchairs could walk with crutches, and those who originally needed 2 crutches now used only one crutch.

Before the study, 7 patients could manage the necessities of their daily lives, compared with 34 after the study.

Patients were evaluated by commonly used indices of rehabilitation. The treatment was judged to be excellent in 23%, good in 47%, fine in 23%, and bad in 7%. The total effectiveness rate (improvement) was 93%. (Huang Meiguang, The General Hospital of PLA, Beijing, China)

65. Observations of the Therapeutic Effect on Myopia of Teenagers Practicing "Relaxing and Quiescent Qigong for Eyes."

Myopia (nearsightedness) improved in 87% of participants in

the study. (Wu Binjiang, et al, Institute of Acupuncture and Moxibustion, China Academy of Traditional Chinese Medicine, Beijing, China)

67. A Case of Cerebroatrophy Cured by Qigong.

A 79 year old male teacher experienced dizziness, slow thinking, feeling top heavy, and impaired motion. A CAT scan (diagnostic scanning examination) found atrophy (shrinking) of his brain, a common finding in Alzheimer's patients.

After one year of self practice of Qigong, with occasional treatments with emitted qi, he returned to normal. Amazingly, his CAT scan also returned to normal. This could well be the only such reversal ever reported in the medical literature. (Zhao Guang, Xiyuan Hospital, China Academy of Traditional Chinese Medicine, Beijing, China)

76. A Group Observation and Experiment Research on the Prevention and Treatment of Hypertension (high blood pressure) by Qigong.

The study group consisted of 639 patients. Qigong practice was the only treatment used. Eighty-five percent of patients effectively controlled their blood pressure. Of successfully treated patients who continued to practice Qigong, 98% were maintaining good control of their blood pressure one year later. (Li Ziran, et al, Research Institute of TCM, Tianjin College of TCM, Tianjin, China)

89. A Study of Qigong in Treatment of Impotence and Its Wonderful Efficiency.

A Taiwan practitioner of Qigong claimed such wonderful results in the treatment of impotency, he offered to refund medical fees to anyone who experienced a treatment failure. Unfortunately, no statistics were provided. (Huang Chengmo, Director, Unique Culture Features Service of Inner Strength Skill, Taiwan)

109. Measurement and Analysis of The Infrasonic Waves From The Emitted Qi.

Infrasonic waves are frequencies below 20 Hertz (cycles per second). Emission of infrasonic waves was measured from the laogong energy point (P 8). Energy emitted by Qigong masters was 100 times that of non-masters. (Niu Xin, et al, Beijing College of Traditional Chinese Medicine, Beijing, China)

ABSTRACTS OF SELECTED PAPERS FROM THE SECOND WORLD CONFERENCE FOR ACADEMIC EXCHANGE OF MEDICAL QIGONG, BEIJING, CHINA, SEPTEMBER, 1993
Numbers used are those used in the collection of abstracts.

Non-Human Studies

1-31. A Study of the Biological Effect of the Emitted Qi on Microbes.

76% of staphylococcus aureus organisms (bacteria) were killed after an 8 minute exposure to emitted qi. Kill rate was higher than with the disinfectant carbolic acid.
Kill rates varied according to the organism. Kill rates were 42% on bacillus species, and 73% on non-bacillus species. (Liu Zirong, et al, Microbiology Department, Shandong University, Yuanji Study Research Institute, E Zhou, Hubei Province, China)

1-32. A Comparative Study of the Emitted Qi and Physical-Chemical Factors on the Protoplasmic Mutagenesis of Microminospora Echinospora

An organism was treated with emitted qi. Death rates were 86%

at 5 minutes, and 92% at 8 minutes. Surviving organisms showed a 75% mutation rate. (Liu Zirong, et al, Dept. of Microorganism, Shandong University Yuan Study Research Institute. E Zhao, Hubei Province, China)

1-33. The Repeated Experiments by Using the Emitted Qi in Treatment of Spinal Cord Injury

Eighteen small test pigs were divided into three groups. All were given a spinal cord injury by "Allen's" method. This stretching method produced a paraplegia (paralysis of the legs) in all of the animals. The first two groups (A and B) were treated with Ba Gua Induction Qigong two to three times a day. The third group served as a control.

After 89 days of treatment all 6 pigs in group A could walk. Five pigs out of 6 in group B could walk. No pigs in group C (untreated) could walk. (Wan Sujian, et al, Qigong Institute, Beijing Military Region, Hebei Langfarg People's Hospital, Beijing Agricultural University)

1-38. Protective Effect of the Emitted Qi on the Cultured Neurons of Neurocytes in Vitro After Free Radical Damage

Nerve cells from newborn rats were cultured in dishes and exposed to damage by the hydroxyl free radical (a free radical is a molecule that contains an unpaired electron and this makes it highly reactive and damaging to tissue). Preparations treated with emitted qi showed much less damage than controls. It was concluded that emitted qi may act as a scavenger (destroyer) of hydroxyl free radical. (Hong Qingtao, et al, Institute of Qigong Science, Beijing College of T.C.M., Beijing, China)

1-46. The Emitted Qi on Mice Cancer, Prevention and Treatment

Thirty mice were divided into three equal groups. Before transferring cancers to the mice, groups two and three were treated with emitted qi for two weeks. After transferring cancers, group three was treated for an additional two weeks. All mice were killed at the same time and examine.

It was found that emitted qi decreased the incidence of cancer. In addition, persistent treatment with emitted qi (group three) was found to inhibit cancer growth. (Feng Li-da, et al, Chinese Immunology Research Center, Beijing, China)

Human Studies

2-10. A Clinical Study of the Routine Treatment of Cancer Coordinated by Qigong

Sixty-two intermediate and advanced cancer patients were divided into two equal groups. Patients in both groups were treated with chemotherapy. Those in group I also practiced Qigong exercises.

Patients in group 1 did far better than those in group 2 who did not practice Qigong. Side effects from chemotherapy were minimized and only 8% stopped because of problems. White blood counts remained stable in the Qigong group.

In the control group (no Qigong) 39% stopped chemotherapy because of side effects, and most experienced a decline in the white blood cell count.

The authors pointed out that Qigong therapy can also shrink cancer, and even *cure* cancer. A case report was presented. A man was seen in 1985 with advanced cancer of the esophagus. He was treated with a combination of chemotherapy and Qigong. He was alive and tumor free 8 years later (cancer of the esophagus is almost uniformly fatal, and seldom is affected by chemotherapy). (Wang Shouzhanga, et al, Henan Tumor Hospital Institute, Zhengzhou, China)

2-11. Curative Effect Analysis of 122 Tumor Patients Treated by the Intelligence-Qigong

Qigong treatment was used in 122 patients with benign and malignant tumors. Of 51 patients with recurrent cancer, 33 were investigated and seventeen of them died. Those who died did so without suffering.

It was concluded that Intelligence Qigong is useful for treating tumors. The survivors live better, while the "unsurvivors" died without suffering. (Zhao Hongmei, et al, The Hospital of The East Lake, Wuhan, China)

2-21. A Clinical Study of the Anti-Aging Effect of Qigong

Super-oxide dismutase (SOD) was measured in two groups of retired females. In a group practicing Qigong, the red cell level of SOD was 2,718.15 plus or minus 593.6 u/g Hemoglobin. In the control group the level of SOD was 1,704.3 plus or minus 572.84 u/g Hemoglobin.

Super-oxide dismutase is an enzyme made in the body that scavanges (destroys) the super-oxide free radical. The super-oxide free radical is one of many factors implicated in the aging process. (Xu Hefen, et al, Jiangsu Provincial Institute of TCM, Nanjing, China)

2-25. Preliminary Observations of 9 Cases of Sjogren's Syndrome Treated Mainly by "Kong Jing Gong"

Sjogren's syndrome is an auto-immune disease of unknown cause with no known effective treatment in either Western medicine or TCM. Nine female cases were studied who had Sjogren's syndrome from 2 to 17 years. With Qigong practice, 2 cases became free of symptoms. Another case improved markedly. Six others improved to some degree. (Yue Zhaosheng, et al, Affiliated with

Dong Zhi Men Hospital, Beijing College of TCM, Beijing, China)

A NURSING HOME STUDY OF THE CHOW INTEGRATED HEALING SYSTEM

Dr. Chow participated in a 6 month study at the Columbia Lutheran Home (a nursing home) in Seattle, Washington, in 1985 and 1986, and test patients experienced amazing responses. The overall plan was to evaluate the Chow Integrated Healing System in nursing home patients.

The first step was the training of 11 key staff members of the nursing home who received 100 hours of instruction from Dr. Chow. These 11 staff members then trained an additional 19 staff members in an 18 hour program under Dr. Chow's supervision. Aspects in the training program included the following:

1)   Proper posture and breathing with the diaphragm.
2)   Special exercises - Qigong.
3)   Frequent hugs.
4)   Visualization.
5)   Meditation.
6)   Positive reinforcement.
7)   Verbalized affirmation.
8)   Modified Dr. Chow tracking.

As an integral part of this training program Dr. Chow treated five patients in the nursing home for one hour each to demonstrate potentials of The Chow System. The exciting results of these treatment sessions are summarized below:

1. 76 year old male with Parkinson's disease for 10 years. This man had a loss of sensation in the lower extremities, a foot drop, and used a walker. He took large doses of aspirin for severe pain in the left side of his head, and spoke with a staccato-type speech with severe

stuttering.

At the end of the one hour treatment he said he could feel his lower extremities again, was easier to understand with less stuttering, and his use of aspirin decreased.

2. 83 year old female with herpes zoster of the rib cage with residual pain in her shoulder and arm, and addiction to methadone. This woman lay on her side in the fetal position, and had been unable to sit up straight nor lie on her back for several years. Her behavior was demanding and negative, so disruptive she had to be moved from room to room frequently because other patients complained of her behavior. She also caused stress-related problems (burn-out) in personnel of the nursing home. Staff members requested changes in their schedules to avoid being around this woman.

After the one hour treatment her pain was 100% gone, she stopped complaining, sat up straight, no longer lay in the fetal position, and was much easier to care for. She did not need to be moved to a new room again, and staff problems related to this woman ceased.

3. 82 year old female with severe rheumatoid arthritis and degenerative joint disease who hadn't walked for 2 to 3 years. All of her joints were swollen and painful, she couldn't feed herself, nor close her hands into fists. After the first session she was free of pain, could move her left arm above her shoulder, feed herself, and make fists.

4. 78 year old female with Parkinson's disease. This woman complained of a tremor (shaking) of the head, and constant pain. She had vertigo (dizziness), and could not walk without assistance. With a walker and help she could walk only 25 to 50 feet. Her recent memory also was poor.

After the first session, her pain was 100% gone, and she walked independently more than 200 feet. Her mind was clearer, and she was able to recall recent events. She stopped complaining of vertigo, and no longer asked for pain medication.

5. 69 year old female with Alzheimer's disease. This woman was hostile, aggressive, agitated, wandered into other patients' rooms, and occasionally ran out of the facility. Large doses of injectable Valium were required to calm her down. In the treatment session she was well behaved and the Valium injection was not needed, a dramatic improvement in her behavior.

The results from just one hour of treatment from Dr. Chow were so dramatic they later were discussed in testimony presented at the Hearing on Medicare and Acupuncture before the Select Committee on Aging, House of Representatives, Ninety Eighth Congress.

Fifteen suitable patients were selected by the Director of Nursing and Dr. Chow to be participants in the full scale study. Subjects in the experimental group ranged in age from 40 to 94. All of these patients were expected to remain in a permanent care facility due to the nature of their disabilities. All were expected to deteriorate with time, as nursing home patients routinely do. The research was carried out with a sub-control group at the same nursing home, and a comparable control group in a nearby facility.

Dr. Chow flew to Seattle every 4 weeks on weekends to treat each of these 15 patients for 1 hour, and continued this schedule for 6 months. Between Dr. Chow's visits, staff members continued aspects of the program in which they were trained.

Patients received medical evaluations at the beginning of the study, and upon its conclusion. Evaluation forms and questionnaires were completed by staff members. An individual video tape record was made for each patient. All of the 1 hour treatment sessions with Dr. Chow were recorded on video tape, 1 tape for each patient. Such dramatic results occurred during these 1 hour sessions, staff called them *Quantum Leaps*.

Results far exceeded original expectations and goals. Presented here is a brief summary of the 15 study patients and their results, as excerpted from notes written by the nursing director, and the administrator of the nursing home:

1. Karl, male, age 55. (Described in Chapter 10 in more detail) Parkinson's disease, wheel chair bound.

Study improvements: Eliminated drooling, began dancing and jogging, improved speech. Moved out of the nursing home after the 4th visit with Dr. Chow.

2. Lola, female, age 75. Paranoid schizophrenia, with tardive dyskinesia (involuntary movements usually caused by drug therapy), arthritis.

Study improvements: Improved posture, better attitude, able to eliminate medication, helping others, able to play the piano normally again, reduction in temper outbursts, less paranoia, decrease in involuntary movement, total relief of joint pains.

3. Walter, male, age 89. Friedreich's ataxia, diabetes, palsy, wheelchair bound.

Study improvements: Regained ability to use a glass and drink without spilling, ability to sign his name, able to feed himself without being messy, disappearance of verbal stutter or slur, improved personal hygiene, ambulating independently with help of railing.

4. Roy, male, age 86. Degenerative joint disease, depression. Wheel chair restricted.

Study improvements: Cooperative, smiling, can now raise legs independently to place feet on foot rest of wheelchair, improved control of temper, improved hearing, now tries to stand with weight on his feet, can now raise left upper extremity to 100 degrees and touch top of head with hand, improvement in self esteem and attitude, can raise knees to chest with self assistance, now reading one book a week.

5. Louella, female, age 82. Parkinson's disease, hearing loss, forgetfulness, and disorientation. Injured one arm 60 years previously and has never been able to raise it higher than shoulder height.

Study improvements: Marked decrease of tremors of upper extremities, able to ambulate independent of walker, able to self groom as a result of ability to raise upper extremities over head, improved mental functions with decreased forgetfulness, able to stand on tiptoes and do knee bends, improved gate, reduced Parkinsonian shuffle, reduced water retention, significant reduction in post-nasal drip, decreased medication.

6. Elmer, Male, age 77. Post stroke. Partially paralyzed in left leg and arm. Hostility.

Study Improvements: Can extend left upper extremity over head, raises arms and legs well, improved ambulation, good posture and breathing, improved attitude.

7. Lillian, female, age 77. Diabetes, agitation, jaw tightness, degenerative joint disease.

Study Improvements: Improved joint function, increased relaxation, improved speech, improved memory, decreased rigidity of the neck, improved posture, decreased pain.

8. Anna, female, age 88. Osteoporosis, poor memory.

Study improvements: Increased alertness and memory, increased range of motion in fingers with less stiffness, increased flexibility of arms, happier attitude, not getting lost in the halls of the nursing home, good posture, less frequent back pain, improved arm extension.

9. Mabel, female, age 94. Degenerative joint disease.

Study improvements: Independently ambulatory with cane, decreased sensitivity of legs, good posture, improved balance, reduction in pain without medication.

10. Kay, female, age 61. Multiple Sclerosis needing full assistance.

Study improvements: Range of motion improved, improved use of left arm -- can raise left arm above head with help of right arm, able to dress and undress with only minimal assistance, complexion cleared, pleasant attitude, can now turn self over independently.

11. Ellen, female, age 86. Dementia, wheelchair bound.

Study improvements: Improved memory, attitude, posture and ambulation, follows directions well, ambulates with walker, improved awareness, can now extend arms up well, increased strength, some relief of eye strain.

12. Olga, female, age 84. Early Dementia, wheelchair bound.

Study improvements: Decreased water retention, can now raise upper extremities over head, shoulders more relaxed, out of wheelchair, resolution of knee swelling, no complaint of pain, does straight leg lifts and knee raises well, ambulates to all activities, improved gait, can now tie her own shoe laces, increase in alertness, positive attitude.

13. Paul, male, age 83. Diabetes, aphasia (unable to speak), wheelchair bound.

Study Improvements: Improved posture, follows directions well, improved self-image, decreased depression, can now raise both arms 180 degrees, wearing dress shoes (instead of slippers), cutting own meat at meals, walks without shuffle for sixty feet, can button and unbutton shirt and remove sweater.

14. Elizabeth, female, age 40. Multiple Sclerosis of 19 years. Total assistance required.

Study improvements: Spasm considerably decreased upon raising arms above head, turns over independently with ease and increased speed, tremor on left side decreased, speaks slower and clearer, very positive and happy, turned forty-three times on mat with better control and smoothness, decrease in all tremors, regained some sensation in both legs, able to recite entire alphabet in one breath, able to bring legs up to chest using belt, good posture returned, able to drink from a cup without spilling, can now sit without support.

15. Edla, female, age 93. Osteoporosis, Parkinson's Disease, wheelchair restricted.

Study improvements: Can do Precious Eight routines well, head shaking much less, walking by self fairly steadily, no observable head shaking while walking, improved circulation of hands and feet, was able to discontinue acetaminophen for pain, lower back pain gone, good mobility of ankle, positive attitude, can raise knees to hand rails, balance and endurance improved, good control of tremors, able to remember Dr. Chow's name, can now ambulate all over the building independently, no longer using wheel chair.

Other surprising healings occurred during the 6 months of the study. One of the patients in the above study group of 15 was wheelchair bound and shared a room with her sister who was paralyzed on one side from a stroke. The sister with the stroke was not in the study, but learned how to do Qigong exercises and supportive measures from her sister. Both sisters regained the ability to walk! It was quite remarkable to see them because their legs were thin, frail, and spindly from disuse.

The man in charge of maintenance at the hospital participated in the 100 hour course and participated in the research program. It turned out that this man had a natural ability to heal with his hands. He treated several patients and was able to feel disturbed energies with his hands. He learned to "brush away" energy disturbances and relieve pain.

One patient who could not ambulate by herself was able to walk after the man in charge of the maintenance department treated her for 5 minutes. Another woman had a headache problem as well as noticeable inflammation and swelling in a thumb. After only 3 minutes of treatment the swelling in the thumb was gone and the woman reported her headache had gone away as well.

After this project was completed, the Nursing Director of the nursing home made the following comments.

"The project has been a very rewarding experience. It is exciting to see the responses of clients: the improved self-esteem, attitude, support of each other and love. The training that the staff has received is invaluable and certainly challenging to the nursing profession. We're truly excited. We feel like pioneers on a new threshold of health."

AN ACCURATE MEASUREMENT OF MUSCLE STRENGTH AND THE EFFECT OF QI. Sancier, Kenneth, and Chow, Effie Poy Yew, *American Journal of Acupuncture* 1991;19:367-377.

Dr. Kenneth Sancier (of the Qigong Institute/East West

Academy of Healing Arts) devised a means of accurately measuring the amount of force a tester applies to the arms of a person being tested, as well as the response over time. The test subjects stood on an electronic digital scale that was connected to a computer. Dr. Chow's hands were attached to a cord that passed upward over a resistance potentiometer, also connected to the computer. Therefore, as she pushed down on subjects' hands any and all variations in force and arm length could be monitored.

Before each test session a card was drawn at random from a stack of cards. Each card had a different sequence of the letters W, for weak, and S for strong. These cards could be seen only by Dr. Chow. For example, a card might have the sequence I (for initial strength test), W, W, S, W, S.

Before each arm muscle test of a subject, the examiner (Dr. Chow) performed a nonverbal Qigong maneuver by emitting her qi to alter the qi of the subject with the intent of altering the subject's body energy. The subject was asked to stand with arms extended, one hand over the other, palms facing down, with hands at forehead level. The subject was asked to resist a downward force of increasing magnitude applied by the examiner's hands for about 4 seconds.

After about 15 seconds another Qigong maneuver was made and another measurement taken. A total of 6 measurements were made for each of 8 subjects of both sexes who were between 30 to 60 years of age and had no apparent health problems. All were members of a Qigong class.

The subjects were admitted one at a time to a room containing the measuring equipment. They were not informed of the intention or interpretation of the experiment. There was no verbal communication between Dr. Chow and the subjects during the measurements. Subjects were asked not to discuss the procedures with others who were still to be tested.

Three variables were measured for each arm muscle test: 1. The downward force that was gradually exerted on the subject's hands; and 2. The height of the hands; 3. The time a subject could resist the downward force was determined from the time required to lower the subject's arms. Analysis of the data showed subjects became weaker or stronger according to the intent and actions of Dr. Chow.

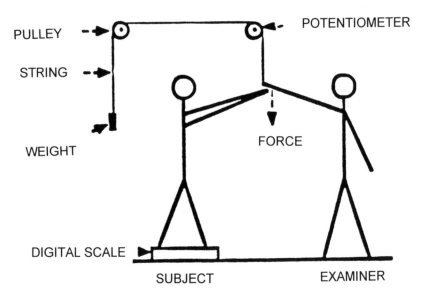

Figure 4. Stick drawing representing set up of experiment.

RESEARCH ON "ANTI-AGING" EFFECT OF QIGONG
Kuang, Ankun, et. al., *Journal of Traditional Chinese Medicine* 1991;11(2):153-158, 1991.   Shanghai Institute of Hypertension, Shanghai Second Medical University, Shanghai.

In a series of studies, involving various tests, improvements were demonstrated in patients' health through Qigong practice. Patients with high blood pressure who practiced Qigong maintained lower readings on a long term basis than did controls who did not practice Qigong (all patients received low doses of hypotensive drugs).

Sex hormone levels were normalized in the elderly.   The incidence of retinopathy was diminished (deterioration of the inside of the back of the eye which can lead to blindness). EKGs improved in 52% of Qigong practitioners, compared to only 22% of controls.

Heart function improved. After one year, cardiac output measurements increased in the Qigong group. Blood viscosity (thickness) decreased, and platelet aggregation (a measurement of the tendency for platelets to stick together and form clots) decreased. In addition, blood levels of HDL-C increased. All of these are desirable changes that generally do not improve with age.

Blood sugar levels improved in different group of patients with diabetes. Before these patients learned Qigong, their average fasting blood sugar was 171 mg/dl. After practicing Qigong for six months, their average fasting blood sugar was 151 mg./dl.

A STUDY OF THE RECUPERATION FUNCTION OF QIGONG ON HYPERTENSION TARGET ORGAN IMPAIRMENT
Xu, Dinghai, et. al., *Journal of Clinical Cardiology* 1992;8(2):66.
Shanghai Institute of Hypertension, Shanghai 200025, China.

86 people with a 10 to 20 year history of high blood pressure were studied. All were on Western drugs and had diastolic (lower) blood pressures of over 95 mm. of mercury (consistent readings over 90 mm. of mercury are taken to indicate high blood pressure). Measurements were made at the beginning of the study, and after one year of Qigong practice.

Ejection fractions improved from an average of 49% to 57% (ejection fraction is a measurement of the efficiency of the pumping action of the heart). EKGs improved. Patients had improved brain function, as measured by isoelectric statistical mapping analysis. Albumin spill in the urine decreased by 50%. All of these improvements are highly unusual.

MEDICAL APPLICATIONS OF QIGONG AND EMITTED QI ON
HUMANS, ANIMALS, CELL CULTURES, AND PLANTS:
REVIEW OF SELECTED SCIENTIFIC RESEARCH
Sancier, Kenneth M., Binkun Hu, *American Journal of Acupuncture*
1991;19(4):367-377.

This report contains selected studies that were reported during
two international conferences on Qigong. All of the studies reported
measurable effects of emitted qi and were felt to have been conducted
with good scientific methodology, according to the standards of
Western science.

QIGONG AND BRAIN WAVES AS RECORDED BY THE EEG
Liu Guo-Long, et. al., Beijing College of TCM. Presented at the First
International Congress of Qigong at the University of California,
Berkeley, 1990.

Dr. Liu is a Western trained neurophysiologist. He says he
began to study the effects of Qigong with the intent of exposing it to
be nothing more than the result of hypnotic suggestion. He studied
14 people who practiced Qigong and, 45 untrained people.
Dr. Liu took EEGs (brain wave tracings) of all subjects while
they were in a relaxed state. EEGs of practitioners of Qigong
demonstrated stronger alpha waves than untrained people (alpha
waves increase during the meditation state). When untrained people
were receiving emitted qi from a Qigong master they also showed
stronger alpha waves. In addition, while receiving emitted qi, their
EEGs showed a synchronization of brain waves with the Qigong
master who was emitting qi.
Many of his colleagues remained skeptical, so he conducted
additional human experiments. He took EEGs of untrained subjects
while they were being treated with emitted qi from real Qigong
masters, and also when they were exposed to pseudo-Qigong masters
who copied the movements of the Qigong masters. The EEGs

changed only in response to treatment from the real Qigong masters.

This still did not satisfy his critics, so he conducted additional experiments in animals to eliminate possible psychological influences. Liu carried out EEG experiments on awake rabbits and Acoustical Brainstem Evoked Response studies (ABER) in anesthetized cats. Shifts in EEG and ABER occurred in animals treated with emitted qi that were similar to those observed in human subjects. In these experiments psychological factors were clearly absent, and Dr. Liu now is an outspoken proponent of Qigong. (Abstracted from an essay by Dr. Kenneth Sancier of the Qigong Institute, East West Academy of Healing Arts, and the China Healthways Newsletter, March 1994)

Chapter 9: SOME PROMINENT QIGONG MASTERS

"There are no unnatural or supernatural phenomena, only very large gaps in our knowledge of what is natural...We should strive to fill those gaps of ignorance."

Edgar D. Mitchell
Apollo 14 Astronaut

A SPECIALIST IN THE TREATMENT OF STROKES

Because of the nature of Dr. Kong's position and connections, he occasionally receives contact from little known Qigong masters. Some have come out of centuries of secrecy, such as Master Lu in Qinhuangdao; some have discovered a breakthrough in the treatment of a specific disease.

In 1991, a TCM doctor named Wang Heng approached Dr. Kong while he was visiting Xian. Dr. Wang said that he had developed a highly successful method of treating patients who had recently suffered strokes. Dr. Kong called friends at a local Western hospital and arranged for the Qigong master to treat three stroke patients who currently were under medical supervision. After three days of Dr. Wang's treatments, two of the three paralyzed patients were walking!

Although Dr. Kong is quite familiar with the achievements of Qigong masters, even he was surprised at such spectacular results. He arranged for Master Wang to move to Haikou, Hainan province, so his capabilities could be studied in a Western hospital affiliated with a medical school.

The study began shortly after the master moved to Hainan. The next 100 acute stroke patients to enter the hospital were referred to him for treatment. A requirement for inclusion in the study was that patients must have had their strokes less than twenty days before beginning the treatment.

Each patient was paralyzed on one side of the body. Wang's treatment consisted of placing six acupuncture needles into energy points in the scalp, points described in the ancient classical literature. After needles were stimulated (twisted) with a new manner developed by Master Wang, qi was transmitted directly into the patient through the needles.

Each patient was treated for only thirty minutes, three days in succession. Incredibly, eighty-five of the one hundred patients were able to walk after only three sessions. Each one of these successful cases could be called a miracle. In the most spectacular case, a man who was five days post-stroke walked immediately after the first treatment. As soon as the needles were removed, he stood up announcing that he wanted to get some fresh air. Totally unassisted, he walked down three flights of stairs and out into a patio!

Wang is sharing the information and teaching his new method to other Qigong masters. Most of the other masters achieve ambulation in their patients about thirty percent of the time. The most likely reason offered for this disparity is that Dr. Wang's qi is probably stronger than that of the other masters. Then again, performing an outright miracle in healing in thirty percent of patients is amazing. If only all of us could do the same.

QIGONG MASTER YAN XIN

While in Beijing in early 1990, the three "honored guests" (Drs. Sancier, Chow, and McGee) met Professor Lu Zuyin of the Institute for High Energy Physics, of the Chinese Academy of Sciences. Dr. Lu was seventy-two at the time, a nuclear physicist, and highly regarded as one of China's top scientists.

To our delight we found that Dr. Lu spoke fluent English. In a relaxed setting over tea he told us about Master Yan Xin and the experiments he had conducted with this Qigong master. Professor Lu began with Yan Xin's background.

Yan Xin was born in Sichuan province in 1950. At the age of four he began to study Qigong with his grandfather. During his training years he studied with over twenty kung fu (martial arts) and Qigong masters, including a famous master named Hai Dung. Simultaneously he continued his academic studies and eventually received a doctor of TCM degree from the University of Chinese Traditional Medicine in Chongqing. In the mid 1980s Yan Xin became a public figure when reports of several of his spectacular cures appeared in the press.

Two of his most famous cases involved patients with serious trauma to the spine. One was a thirty-one year old man who was in a motorcycle accident. X-rays showed he suffered a compression fracture of T-12 (a spinal bone in the lower chest). In a compression fracture a spinal bone is partially crushed, and the defect shows clearly on x-rays.

Yan Xin treated this man with emitted qi daily for forty days. His pains went away quickly, and by the end of the treatment he experienced "complete healing" (as described in *Yan Xin's Scientific Qigong,* China Books Press, 1988).

The second case was more dramatic involving Yang Jixiang, a thirty-six year old man who was injured in a fall at work. Yang suffered a skull fracture, a compression fracture of his L-2 vertebra (in the lower back), and injury to his spinal nerve. Emergency brain surgery was performed to remove a blood clot on his brain, and eight days later bones in his lower back were fused (surgically connected together to produce a stability of the spine). The injury left him paralyzed in both legs, unable to sit up or turn over in bed. Muscles in his legs gradually shrank from disuse (atrophied).

Yan Xin first saw Yang seven months after the accident. After traveling all day and evening, he first examined Yang at about ten in the evening and decided to treat him immediately. Yan Xin asked to be taken to a temple ten miles away and from there he emitted qi at Yang for six consecutive hours, all night, from eleven P.M. to five A.M. During the treatment Yang said he felt warm throughout, and sweated profusely with an aroma of sandalwood. After the treatment, Yang slept for nine hours, When he woke up, to the amazement of everyone, he could walk again. (Case described in *Yan Xin Qigong and the Contemporary Sciences,* International Yan Xin Qigong Association, 1991).

Five months later, on October 7, 1987, Yang and eleven other patients who had experienced miraculous cures, walked far up the Great Wall with Master Yan on national television. Observers noted that Yang walked with only a trace of a limp.

Almost overnight curiosity about Qigong reached a high level and Dr. Yan found himself to be in great demand. Members of Qigong societies all over China invited him to give public speeches, and he frequently lectured to as many as 30,000 people in packed sports arenas. As he did so, he emitted his healing qi to the audience, and this was the principal reason people came to see him. Because of lingering problems with incompatible regional dialects in China, many people in those audiences couldn't understand a word Dr. Yan said, but this did not seem to matter.

During these events many people began to move involuntarily similar to behavior previously described during lectures by Master Lu of Qinhuangdao. Some stood up and walked in place near their seats. Others later claimed to have experienced cures of various ailments during, or immediately after, these appearances. Dr. Yan says that these unusual movements and behaviors occur when qi evokes healing responses in the energies of people in the crowd.

Yan Xin's renown spread and spread. China Central Television produced and broadcast a documentary on him called *Chinese Superman -- Yan Xin,* and this caused his fame to spread even further. Soon, Yan Xin was a familiar name to a billion people.

Professor Lu studied Yan Xin for two years from 1986 to 1988. He told us that before he met Yan Xin he was a total skeptic about Qigong, and did not believe any of the stories that were circulating. He believed that the entire subject amounted to nothing more than exaggeration, superstition, and inaccurate observations.

At this time Yan Xin was saying publicly that he could manipulate physical matter with his qi. Professor Lu's colleagues urged him to perform scientific studies on Yan Xin to see if this were indeed true. Professor Lu was reluctant to waste his time, or be associated with a charlatan, but in the end he agreed. His principal intent in doing so was to demonstrate that Yan Xin's claims were inaccurate exaggerations, with no foundation in fact.

Yan Xin agreed to participate in several experiments. Abstracts of these studies are available in English from the Qigong Institute, East West Academy of Healing Arts (Yan Xin's Scientific Qigong). In every experiment, scientific methodologies were critiqued by other scientists who made every attempt to eliminate the possibility of manipulation and trickery.

Alteration of the Decay Rate of a Radioactive Compound

In preparation for the first study, Professor Lu asked Yan Xin if he could decrease the decay rate of a radio-active compound. To a nuclear physicist, this is the same as asking if human beings can turn off nuclear reactions in the sun. Professor Lu said Yan Xin's reply translated into a simple, "Can do."

Professor Lu selected the radio-active compound Americium-241 for the study because it has a long half life of 458 years and is safe to handle for brief periods of time. The Americium-241 was in the shape of coin shaped slugs, about the size of a medium sized coin. The normal variability in radioactive readings (yield shift) of Americium-241 is only 0.06% per day.

Yan Xin "treated" the slug of Americium-241 from a distance of ten meters for about twenty minutes. Professor Lu then placed the slug in a vertical slot that was placed an equal distance from two detection instruments (computer controlled 8,000-channel recorders that report radioactive emissions digitally). Two counters were used because readings could be altered if a piece of equipment were bumped accidentally. Another slug of Americium-241 was used as a control.

On the first trial, the decay rate of the treated specimen decreased 1.05%, a significant alteration that violated the laws of physics! Readings taken on the control slug were not altered. Professor Lu said he felt as if he had gone into a state of shock because, to a nuclear physicist, this can not happen. In the thorough pattern of an investigator, he continued to take readings on the altered Americium-241 slug and found its decay rate gradually returned to normal, but it took eleven days.

Professor Lu asked Yan Xin if he could decrease the decay rate again. Yan Xin wasn't familiar with the repetition required in scientific studies and surprised Professor Lu when he answered, "No, I've done that already."

Professor Lu was fast thinking and asked Yan Xin if he could *increase* the decay rate instead. Once again the response was, "Can do." Yan Xin treated another radio-active slug, and its decay rate increased by eleven percent!

One day when an experiment was scheduled, Yan Xin was busy elsewhere and phoned to say he would not be able to arrive at Professor Lu's laboratory before it closed. However, he offered to treat the Americium-241 slug from where he was, seven kilometers away. Professor Lu set up the experiment, Yan Xin emitted his qi from that distance, and the results came out the same.

Professor Lu asked Yan Xin if there might be a limiting distance in his ability to affect the Americium-241, and Yan Xin said he didn't think there was. To test this concept, Dr. Yan suggested they try the same experiment the next week when he was going to be lecturing in Canton, 1,250 miles (2,000 km.) to the south.

Yan Xin called Professor Lu the following week from Canton, set up timing for the experiment, and the results came out the same. The study later was repeated when Yan Xin was in Kunming and Chengdu (in southern and southwestern China, respectively). The decay rate always was altered in a direction consistent with Yan Xin's *intent*. However, the amount of variability was not constant.

Variations in the decay rate consistently increased with Yan Xin's distance from Beijing. Throughout the studies, the control slug maintained a normal and constant decay rate.

Before he was through, Professor Lu repeated this experiment with Yan Xin forty times. Except for normally seen minor variations, the results were constant. The decay rate went up or down by ten or eleven percent according to the intent of the Qigong master.

Alteration of a Laser

A second study involved a laser. Yan Xin was asked if he could alter the plane of polarization of laser light by emitting his qi from a distance of ten kilometers, and his answer once again was, "Can do." The experiment was set up, qi was emitted, and the light intensity of the laser fluctuated by as much as ten percent! This study also was repeated many times with the same results.

In additional studies Yan Xin altered the composition of gases in an infrared cell, altered the molecular structure of a directional liquid crystal, and altered the chemical composition of various liquid solutions, as measured by Raman spectroscopy. All of these results violate the laws of physics, which scientists currently believe to be constant.

Professor Lu escorted us through his laboratories describing the methodology of the various studies. We had the opportunity to see his instruments, all of which were state of the art.

Some people have raised the question of what really was being measured in these experiments. Some say that the materials themselves are being altered, as described. Others say that Yan Xin might be affecting the measuring instruments used in the studies. If that is the case, then he must have altered the instruments from 1,200 miles away, but not affected them during the testing of control materials, and he had no way to know when Professor Lu was conducting those phases of the experiment. There is no way to resolve this question, but a central observation remains that, according to the usual laws of physics as normally understood, neither event should be possible.

Several books appeared in the Chinese language describing Yan Xin's scientific studies and healing accomplishments, and he became even more famous. He was invited to Hong Kong to demonstrate his unusual abilities, but during that trip, was unable to repeat any of these feats. Detractors in Hong Kong and elsewhere seemed pleased to have an opportunity to criticize Qigong and Yan Xin. Many organizations went on the attack, and the press declared him to be nothing more than a fraud.

The problem is unresolved whether or not all of these studies can be trusted. Other Qigong masters have duplicated most of the Yan Xin experiments with success, but to our knowledge, not those involving the laser or radioactive compound. Some scientists have raised questions of methodologies used in those two studies. Until the matter is resolved, the safest course of action appears to be to withhold judgement on those two experiments.

QIGONG MASTER LIU HENGSHUN

Qigong Master Liu Hengshun currently is receiving substantial media attention in China. Master Liu is fifty-six years old, is a practicing doctor of TCM, sang in the Chinese opera for many years, and lives in Beijing. When he was only four, his grandparents began his training in the martial arts, and "point touch therapy" Qigong.

Master Liu was invited to become a "National Treasure" by the Chinese government, but declined the honor. When such an honor is accepted, a Qigong master comes under the control of high ranking governmental officials and can no longer decide who to treat. Master Liu chose to remain free to provide a service to common people, as well as to high ranking officials.

In Master Liu's acupoint therapy, qi is transferred through the master's fingers to the patient's energy points. The fundamental principle of the method is to balance Yin and Yang to regulate circulation of the blood, regulate metabolism, balance the endocrine (hormone gland) system, restore internal functions, and improve the immune system, thus promoting a healing response.

Master Liu comes from a long line of practitioners of TCM. His great-great-grandfather was personal physician to Emperor Xing Feng of the Qing Dynasty, and treatment methods have been passed down in the family for five generations.

Master Liu received a degree in chemistry from Beijing University in 1958, and graduated from the Beijing College of Traditional Chinese Medicine in 1964. He has treated over 20,000 patients, including many famous personalities and high ranking government officials including Wang Zhen, formerly Vice Chairman of the People's Republic of China.

One of Master Liu's fortes is the treatment of diabetes. To date he has treated over 250 diabetic patients, including a Mr. Xi Bin Mao, a Japanese businessman from Osaka. Xi Bin Mao's diabetes caused him to go blind at one point, but after treatment by Dr. Liu, his eyesight returned. Dr. Liu is reported to have a high success rate in the treatment of diabetic neuropathy, a progressively degenerating condition in which patients develop numbness and pains in their extremities. One impressive response was in a German woman with diabetic neuropathy who regained feeling in her legs during the first twenty minutes of treatment.

Another patient of Master Liu was Hui Shi Gian, a leader in the chemical industry in Harbin. Mr. Hui was diagnosed as having neuritis (inflammation of the nerves) which slowly progressed to a paralysis. The only neurological function he retained was the ability to speak. He was bedridden, couldn't walk, and required continual nursing care. After being treated by Master Liu daily for two weeks, he could walk, feed himself, and perform normal daily activities.

Another famous case was a seven year old child with leukemia (a blood cancer). After treatment by Dr. Liu all blood abnormalities and signs of the disease disappeared.

Another miracle healing was experienced by Xing Chun Hua, director of the Beijing Farm Bureau, who suffered from abdominal pains and gall stones from 1986 to 1988. The gall stones were diagnosed with x-rays. After only four treatments from Master Liu, the gall bladder expelled all the stones. This was verified in 1990 when Mr. Xing underwent surgery for other problems; his surgeon examined the gall bladder manually and felt no stones.

Master Liu's Qigong is quite effective for weight reduction. In one case a woman came to him who was about four feet ten inches tall and weighed 176 pounds. The obesity complicated her heart and liver problems, and she could barely walk. After twenty days of treatment her weight was 143 pounds, she could climb stairs, and felt much better.

Because of these miraculous results, Master Liu has become famous. He has been the subject of numerous magazine and newspaper articles, and has appeared on television many times. His work demonstrates what Qigong can accomplish at the highest level,

Figure 1. Master Liu treating famous pianist Lao Zi Cheng with acupoint therapy.

as well as the moral integrity of Qigong masters. Master Liu lives modestly, treats most patients in their own homes, and treats the poor for no charge.

QIGONG MASTER SUN YUN CAI

Sun Yun Cai, the master of the Guo Lin school, was born in 1934 into a teacher's family in Nanjing and graduated from the Beijing Teacher's Training College in 1961. She worked at four middle schools in Beijing where she taught Chinese, Chinese History, World History, and attained the title of "Senior Teacher in Beijing."

In 1980, she discovered a 5 by 5 by 3 centimeter lump in her right breast, which was removed and diagnosed as cancer. Her treatment involved removal of both breasts (radical mastectomies), followed by radiation therapy and chemotherapy. However, treatment could not be completed because of a severe drop in her white blood cell count. At that time, x-rays showed the cancer had spread to her right lung, as well as to the right side of her abdominal cavity. Her Western trained physicians discontinued all treatments and considered her condition to be hopeless.

She began to learn "New Qigong" created by Qigong Master Guo Lin. Through advice from Master Guo Lin and assistance from her pupils, Mr. Gao Wen Bin (suffering from advance stages of lung cancer), and Mr. Yu Da Yuan (suffering from advance stages of cancer of the rectum), Ms. Sun soon mastered the skills. She exercised persistently on a daily basis, and also took Chinese herbal medicines. She then learned to swim under Qigong conditions, continued her unremitting efforts for one year, and the cancer disappeared completely.

After her experience, Ms. Sun had great empathy for other cancer patients and began to develop a program of activities to promote a healing response in others. She applied new methods which combine Western medicine, TCM, and Qigong techniques based on a symbiotic synthesis of social sciences and biological sciences.

In 1989, Ms. Sun, Mr. Gao Wen Bin, and Mr. Yu Da Yuan (the previously mentioned seriously ill cancer patients), established the "Beijing Ba Yi Lake Cancer-Resistant Paradise," and the "Beijing Cancer-Resistant Paradise," to make this new treatment method available for large contingents of cancer patients. Elected as the organization's secretary general, Master Sun represented Beijing by participating in the "First Cancer Patients' Olympic Games" in Shanghai during March, 1993.

For over ten years, Master Sun has held annual Guo Lin Qigong seminars at the Yu Yuan Tan Park in Beijing for the benefit of cancer patients from all over China, as well as from overseas. She has been invited to teach Guo Lin Qigong in several Chinese provinces, conducting over 200 seminars attended by over 9,000 people. Concentrating on Qigong theory, a knowledge of Western medicine, TCM, and dietary therapy, she treats patients based on an overall analysis of their illness and condition.

Employing psychological techniques, she practices Qigong on her patients to calm them and prolong their lives, and about 90% of patients improve to some degree. Many advanced cancer patients have survived much longer than their Western trained doctors expected and some have become cancer free.

Master Sun has published various articles such as "Make a Unified Treatment--Be Your Own Master," and also edited the book, "*Cancer Patients Speak of Cancer Resistance*." At the first Guo Lin seminar her speech, "The Psychotherapy of Guo's Values," was well received. She also has published articles titled "Live to Achieve One's Own Values" in *Life Magazine*, as well as "Cancer Does Not Equal Death" in *Women's Life Magazine*, which reported on patients' efforts in their struggle with cancer.

In the book titled *How to Practice Guo Lin Qigong* she elaborates on the theory behind Guo Lin's Qigong. In the "*Cancer Resistance Garden*," she elaborates on the main principles of how Guo Lin Qigong helps patients overcome cancer (all of these

Guo Lin Qigong helps patients overcome cancer (all of these publications are available only in Chinese).

Because of her contributions to Guo Lin Qigong and assistance to patients and fellow cancer sufferers, Master Sun has been well received by the people. She has been visited by social psychologists, doctors, Qigong enthusiasts, and patients from the USA, France, Germany, Singapore, Malaysia, Japan, Taiwan, and Hong Kong. She also has had the opportunity to describe her own recovery and cancer related work on many Chinese television networks, newspapers, and magazines.

Currently Master Sun is the director of the Guo Lin Qigong Research Seminars. She is in good health, full of energy, and swims during the winter in near freezing water. She has dedicated her life to helping fellow cancer patients recover through the methods of Master Guo Lin.

Figure 2. Master Sun (on the right) leading a group of cancer patients in Guo Lin Qigong.

Chapter 10: CASE HISTORIES

"The goal is to develop curiosity about things unknown, the ability to continue learning, the flexibility to adapt."
David Stemple
University of Massachusetts

A WESTERN DOCTOR DISCOVERS QIGONG

I first heard of Qigong when Dr. Stephen Kong visited my home in 1987. I was asked to be a medical consultant on several of his projects because of my long term involvement in alternative medicine. Later that year I visited Beijing for the first time. I had heard of the high level martial arts form of (hard) Qigong, but knew nothing of medical, or soft, Qigong. Unable to arrange a viewing of hard Qigong, Dr. Kong took me to the apartment of a surgeon who introduced me to a seventy year old Western trained physician named Li Lau-Shi. Dr. Li was famous in medical circles in Beijing because of a truly miraculous cure he experienced in a hospital directly under the surveillance of Western-trained colleagues and friends.

Dr. Li became paralyzed below the waist at the age of thirty-five (most likely from polio) and practiced Western medicine from a wheelchair for the next fifteen years. During that time his health deteriorated progressively as he developed several other serious health problems. Li's vision was so poor he had to wear heavy, thick, corrective glasses. His blood pressure gradually rose to dangerous levels, high enough to threaten a stroke. He took a series of Western drugs for his high blood pressure: none helped. In addition, he began to experience recurrent bouts of pneumonia; these infections led to a series of hospitalizations.

In 1957, at the age of fifty, Li was hospitalized with another bout of severe bilateral pneumonia. His doctors tried one new wonder antibiotic after another but there was no response. He was weakening and his temperature continued to rise until it hovered around 105 degrees (F). At that point his specialists bluntly told him to get his affairs in order and say good-bye to his loved ones because he was going to die.

Li Lau-Shi did not accept this forecast of his impending demise. He had recently begun to practice Qigong and in desperation intensified his practice efforts. He made a serious effort to practice as instructed, spending all of his waking hours doing Qigong exercises lying flat on his back in bed.

Defying his doctors' pessimistic predictions, Li slowly began to improve. During the next year, he made a complete recovery from the lung infections. His blood pressure gradually returned to normal without any medications. His vision slowly improved and eventually he no longer needed corrective glasses at all. The most impressive improvement was in his paralysis. During the year he slowly regained the ability to walk normally again.

When I met Dr. Li twenty years later, he appeared to be in excellent health. His cheeks were full and smooth; he was agile, coordinated, and appeared to be about twenty years younger than his chronological age. After his recovery he gave up practicing medicine and taught Qigong. Every morning he rode a bus to a neighborhood park in Beijing to give free instructions to about 200 students.

This kind of story is difficult for a Western trained physician to believe. I discovered there was no place in my brain for the information to be assimilated. It just didn't compute, just as much of this book won't compute in the minds of other Western physicians.

By that time (1987) I had been involved in alternative therapies for thirteen years, studying acupuncture and TCM since 1974. However, I found many of the theories of TCM pushed my belief system too far. During my initial acupuncture course, I sat in the front row during lectures on such things as the Law of Five Elements, time clocks of energy flow, mother/son relationships, yin and yang, etc. One teacher singled me out of 300 physicians saying, "We have a smirker in the front row." Over several years, I accepted most of the theories of TCM as valid because patients did so well with treatments. Also, new research appeared.

Now, here was another strange TCM method to contend with, namely Qigong. Success stories following treatment with acupuncture and herbs were common, but they generally involved minor problems such as headaches, aches, and pains. Lacking were stories of miraculous recoveries from untreatable conditions such as paralysis and cancer.

I didn't know what to think about Li's story, and had no way to verify the details. Then again, there was nothing for my hosts to gain by concocting such an improbable tale. Li's recovery didn't fit anything with which I was familiar. I filed the story away somewhere in my mind, never mentioning it to anyone for fear my friends would think I had gone crazy.

The next year I returned to Beijing on other business, unprepared for what happened. Dr. Kong literally pushed me into Qigong and I couldn't understand why. I protested that I didn't fly half way around the world to get involved in something about which I knew nothing.

I had lunch with two Qigong masters whom Dr. Kong employed through his governmental office. One was a woman, North Korean by birth, who had developed breast cancer diagnosed with a needle biopsy ten years previously. After refusing conventional treatments, she selected Qigong as her only therapy and cured herself using Guo Lin Qigong. The other master was Xia Lei-ming, a man about thirty.

Later we went to a friend's apartment to view a documentary on Qigong made in China by a Japanese television network and broadcast in Japan in 1987. Kong's two Qigong masters participated in the production of the tape.

I saw many spectacular things. The paralyzed limbs of two stroke patients flew up in the air in direct response to the actions of a Qigong master (who was not even touching them). One young man with lung cancer cured his disease through the use of Qigong exercises alone. Many research studies were described including one in which emitted qi killed bacteria (as shown by a comparison of culture plates). Another study showed electronmicroscopic photos of cancer cells (in tissue culture) that were killed with emitted qi. Each of these events was miraculous all by itself.

Later, I saw Master Xia treat a sixty year old man who had been paralyzed in both arms and legs for eighteen months following a stroke. After only ten minutes into the first treatment, the man shuffled slowly around the room without assistance.

Dr. Kong told me that the Chinese government accepted Qigong as being a real phenomenon and was eager to share its benefits with the world. I saw no reason for my Chinese hosts to fabricate what they were showing me. As I witnessed and became aware of many miraculous healings through the use of Qigong, I finally accepted it as a truly miraculous discovery.

After returning home I was determined to find out if Qigong had arrived in the West and it didn't take long to find Dr. Chow. We became friends and agreed to collaborate to make Westerners aware of the miraculous potential of Qigong. This led to our discovery trip to China in 1990 (Chapter 4) and to the scheduling of a Qigong seminar near my home later in the year.

RELEASED TENDONS

Dr. Chow visited my area in 1990 to present a weekend class in Qigong. One evening she and I were working on a project in my office when my twenty year old son-in-law dropped by. After introducing Dr. Chow to Dennie, I asked her to take a look at his left hand.

Dennie had severed the tendons of the fourth and fifth fingers (in the palm) of his left hand in a job-related accident about two years previously. A hand surgeon sewed the tendons back together and a course of physical therapy followed. The long-term result was that the two fingers stayed in a partially contracted position. They could not be flattened like the others.

When Dr. Chow saw Dennie's deformed fingers, she looked as if she could hardly wait to get her hands on them. She held Dennie's fingers between her hands, and seemed to massage them, but I knew more was going on. Dennie began to turn beet red all over and to sweat profusely. His tee-shirt rapidly became soaked with sweat.

After about five minutes, Master Chow stopped working with Dennie's fingers and tested their mobility. As if by magic, both previously contracted fingers were straightened out to a normal position. Dennie didn't know what to think and Dr. Chow beamed with pleasure. However, she told Dennie he must learn Qigong exercises and needed more treatments to maintain the improvement.

When Dr. Chow noticed that I didn't seem to be as thrilled about Dennie's response as she was, she looked disappointed. I told her miracles had become so routine I was more surprised when one did not occur.

I asked Dr. Chow what she experiences when applying healing energy. She said that when she emits Qigong energy, the body part being treated slowly begins to soften up and feels as soft as putty in her hands. Gradually she can mold and move it, changing its shape.

MY SON DISCOVERS QI

During her visit to our area, Master Chow came to my home. My son Thom was twenty-two years old, weighed 230 pounds, and worked out lifting weights.

When I introduced Thom to Dr. Chow and told him she could push him anywhere she wished, he looked at us and laughed. It seemed impossible that anyone so petite could do what I described. He thought it was a useless exercise, but agreed to a demonstration.

We went into the back yard where Dr. Chow asked Thom to brace himself with one foot well behind his body while she tried to push him backwards. Confidently, he positioned himself. Dr. Chow pushed against Thom and found him to be as solid as a rock. She then stepped back and performed a Qigong maneuver. Thom braced himself again but this time there was no contest. Dr. Chow pushed him backwards a full forty feet.

Thom's face was red with embarrassment and surprise. No longer a skeptic, he said that when she pushed him the second time, he suddenly felt weak. He couldn't figure out how someone less than half his weight could push him around like that.

On our trip to China earlier in the year, Dr. Chow demonstrated this same routine. The "victim" that time had been Yuan Rujie, a stocky martial arts Qigong performer who also weighed about 200 pounds. When I think of Rujie, I remember the first time I saw him on video tape. With apparent ease, he bent a thick piece of steel around his forearm twice! He had the confident appearance of a strong-man in the circus.

Dr. Chow had no problem doing the same thing to Rujie as she had done to Thom (and anybody else on whom she demonstrates this maneuver). Rujie braced himself, but quickly found he was being pushed backwards into a wall. Simultaneously, his entire family began to chatter in Mandarin, not believing what they saw.

OTHER MIRACLE CASES OF QIGONG

Multiple Sclerosis

Ellen, a cellist for a major symphony orchestra, developed neurologic symptoms in 1976. By 1987, the diagnosis of multiple sclerosis was confirmed. When she first saw Dr. Chow in September of 1988, she couldn't drive a car, play the cello or even walk by herself. When she tried to walk, she had to hang on tightly to her husband's arm and stabilize herself with a cane. Ambulating caused severe spasms in her leg, which led her physician to recommend that she begin using a wheel chair in July, 1988.

After her first treatment with Dr. Chow, she was able to balance by herself and walked out of the building without the use of the cane or assistance from her husband. After two months of therapy she drove to San Francisco and back home by herself, a ninety minute drive each way when traffic is minimal.

She began to hike around by herself and practice her cello again. By Christmas, she and her mother, a cellist with another major symphony orchestra, played a duet concert at a San Francisco hospital. She continued to improve and became the coach of her son's baseball team. After nine months she resumed playing with the symphony and was able to carry her own cello.

In 1994, six years later, she still performs for the symphony, and has traveled to perform in other places as far away as Mexico. As a side project, she started her own symphony orchestra that plays for special occasions and for visiting artists from other countries.

A Stroke Case

Mary's healing demonstrates another example of the wonders of Qigong. A sixty-two year old woman from North Carolina, Mary had a stroke two years previously that left her paralyzed on the right side. According to the observations of Western medicine, some stroke patients do regain the use of functions they have lost. However, progress usually stops after six to twelve months. Any paralysis or loss of function present at that time is considered to be permanent.

Mary wore a sling on her shoulders and braces on her right arm and leg. She had been told she would neither drive nor walk again, and that she should begin to use a wheelchair. Her doctor told her never to take off the braces or sling. She used a walker, but couldn't move herself more than six feet at a time. She was tired, very depressed, and represented a real challenge. She very much wanted to be treated by Dr. Chow but could stay for therapy in California for only nine days.

Fortunately, Mary responded to treatment very well. By the end of the first session she took off her sling and braces and walked around without them. She only used them as a precautionary measure when she felt she might need them to make sudden moves.

After nine days of treatment she was able to drink with steady hands. She could move both of her arms up over her head and balance well: she could walk seven blocks up and down the hilly streets of San Francisco. She had good stamina, was no longer depressed and wore a big smile on her face most of the time.

After returning home to North Carolina, Mary continued to practice what she had learned, calling Dr. Chow on several occasions to receive "distant healing." Later, she reported on her progress, sending a picture of herself hoeing her garden. She was walking all around town, passed her driver's test, and was driving "all over the place." She and her family were as happy as could be.

Stroke

Gretchen suffered a series of strokes in the late 1980s. She had been bedridden for several years, unable to care for herself, and her condition was deteriorating. Her husband wanted Dr. Chow to treat her, and a physician was asked to document her condition before and after treatment.

The pre-treatment examination report described Gretchen as drooling constantly and coughing up phlegm, requiring suctioning of her throat day and night. Her entire body was stiff, her contracted arms and legs could not be moved or straightened, and her head could not be moved or turned. She had been fed through a stomach tube for several years.

The post-treatment examination was performed two weeks after therapy with Dr. Chow from November 15th to 30th, 1993. She had improved immediately and her throat had not required suctioning since the first treatment. After the second treatment the drooling stopped and she was sleeping through the night for the first time in years. Her formerly contracted arms and legs became loose and could be straightened out.

She could sit for a short period balancing herself on the bed with her legs over the side. She was still unable to speak, but could make audible sounds and was making facial expressions with her eyes wide open. Her head could move to both sides. She was obviously more alert and responsive. The consulting physician recorded that her overall condition was remarkably improved after only two weeks of Qigong therapy.

Cancer

Allen was fifty-seven years old and dying of cancer (adenoid mucinous carcinoma) when he first saw Dr. Chow in May, 1988. By the time the cancer was discovered, it had spread into his liver and stomach. At exploratory surgery Allen's doctors took some tissue samples to establish a diagnosis and then closed him up.

When he came for Qigong treatment, he had yellow eye balls and skin (jaundice) from liver involvement. His abdomen and liver were enlarged and hard and he had not been eating for some time. His only nourishment was one-half cup of a commercial liquid food product per day, and the lack of fiber caused him to become extremely constipated. His energy level was low and he was extremely depressed which was not at all surprising for a man in his desperate condition. Allen's doctors had scheduled him to begin chemotherapy in two to three weeks.

After the first Qigong treatment, Allen went home and ate an entire bowl of chicken noodle soup and eight crackers. This was the first time in a long while that he had consumed normal food. His appetite improved, he ate more, and within a week his jaundice was almost gone. Over the next two months, his water retention diminished, allowing him to see his ankle bones again. His energy level was higher, he was less depressed, his spirits were improved and his bowels had begun to function normally.

At his first Qigong treatment, he was given special exercises to do which were gentle, yet persistent and vigorous. He continued working with his medical doctor and began chemotherapy three weeks after starting his Qigong program. During chemotherapy he experienced minimal side effects---no nausea, vomiting, or major hair loss. Immediately after each chemotherapy, he had a low energy level and a bad taste in his mouth that lasted for a day or so, but then his energy level picked up again. By Christmas his liver had returned to normal size.

Allen continued doing Qigong exercises for one year. During that time he gained back thirty-six pounds. He was teaching tennis five days a week, ninety minutes each day and walking a great deal. He said that he felt like eating and doing normal activities.

He stated, "My progress was steady and impressive since my first visit with Dr. Chow. At that meeting I weighed 137 pounds soaking wet and couldn't eat more than four ounces of liquid food a day. I had been told by my doctors that they really couldn't help me. Today I weigh 164 pounds and I am eating three solid meals per day, have lots of energy and strength, and am getting better and feeling more wonderful each new day. Ninety-five percent of my improvement and progress has been due to the program I'm following through the East West Academy."

Allen's evaluation of his situation is probably correct because chemotherapy seldom has beneficial effects on his kind of cancer. Allen's cancer never went away, but he was able to reverse the course of his disease with Qigong.

AIDS

Garth was employed in a managerial position by a major airline. He was first diagnosed as HIV positive in 1988, when his T-Cell count was down to 80 (an acceptable level is over 250). When he first saw Dr. Chow in 1989 he was extremely depressed, had no motivation, was very weak, and didn't have the energy to do anything. He was spending a lot of time in bed and preferred to isolate himself from other people. His goal was to become his "good old self."

Garth's blood tests were discouraging. A recent "T-Cell" count was thirty-two, a very low level indicating that his immune system had almost stopped functioning. Fatigue forced him to stop working six weeks earlier: his doctors didn't have anything to offer and had essentially sent him home to die.

Dr. Chow began her Qigong instructions with the breathing and posturing exercises. She had Garth write down a list of positive things about himself and areas in which he felt he needed to improve. On repeat visits he evaluated his rate of improvement in each area.

After his first treatment session with Dr. Chow, Garth reported his energy level had increased about sixty percent. He felt a warm circulation flowing in his body: he was more mentally alert and more like his old self. In his daily log he wrote, "I like myself now."

Garth continued to practice Qigong exercises at home. Within two weeks he was wearing his business suit again and talking about going back to work. He felt like eating again, had gained twenty pounds in just two weeks, and reported that he no longer was depressed. He had tried an experiment to see if he could make himself become depressed but found it was impossible. He was cheerful and laughing when he called to make his next appointment.

Garth began to change his health habits. He cut down his smoking and coffee intake. It didn't take long before he was saying, "The old me is back and I like me."

One month after he first saw Dr. Chow, Garth went back to work. He found he could perform the duties of his job just as well as previously. Unfortunately, a short time after returning to work he stopped doing his exercises. He was able to lead a full life and able to work for another two years before he died. His extended life period is quite an unusual recovery for somebody with that level of T-Cell count.

Garth's sad end demonstrates once more how we have control over our own health. Even potential recovery from a life threatening illness was not enough to motivate him to continue practicing what obviously had been successful. This is in sharp contrast to the actions of Hope, described in Chapter 1.

Parkinson's Disease

Karl was a fifty-five year old man who had lived with Parkinson's disease for a decade. He had been cared for in a nursing home for two years confined to a wheel chair most of the time. He suffered from an unsteady gait, stiff facial muscles, hyperactivity, and limited use of his hands. His left shoulder was permanently raised, his eyes closed, his head leaned to the left, he drooled uncontrollably, and his voice was garbled. When attendants got him up, he walked on the outside of his right foot and needed full assistance.

Dr. Chow treated Karl for the first time in 1984 as part of a research project at the Columbia Lutheran Home, a nursing home in Seattle, Washington (this study is described in Chapter 8). The treatment included relaxation and breathing exercises, massage, positive reinforcement, laughter, hugs, acupressure, and the self-practice of Qigong. Every four weeks, Dr. Chow flew to Seattle to treat each patient for one hour. A video tape was made for each patient to record the treatments with Dr. Chow.

During his first Qigong treatment, Karl opened his eyes normally, the drooling lessened, and he began smiling. By the end of the treatment session, he was able to take a few steps without assistance for the first time in over two years. Karl could feel the results and reacted by shouting loudly, "It's wonderful. It's wonderful"!

Karl slowly graduated from his wheel chair to a walker. He was able to walk to his third Qigong treatment on his own without the walker. By the end of that treatment he was dancing with the nurses. He had loved to dance in the past but had not done so for ten years. The video shows he even "dipped" his partner back, and nobody landed on the floor!

By the end of the fourth Qigong treatment, Karl was able to jog around the room with normal coordination and showed a jovial spirit.

By that time he had been leaving the nursing home to play volleyball with his daughters. He also had begun to flirt with the nurses, occasionally, expressing an embarrassing sexual interest. He had come to life in many ways and his self-esteem was soaring. At that point in his progress, he no longer needed nursing home care and moved out to a boarding home facility.

To prevent any confusion about what might be responsible for his improvement, the daily dose of his Parkinson's medicine (Sinemet) was maintained at a constant level throughout the study period. Anyone who has ever had experience with a far advanced Parkinson's patient will appreciate the miraculous nature of Karl's recovery.

Details of this case were excerpted from notes written by both the Nursing Director and the Administrator of the nursing home. I continue to show the video record of Karl's recovery to patients and other people in my office, and they are amazed because nobody has ever heard of improvement in a patient with Parkinson's disease.

Headaches, Allergies, and Fatigue

"I have been at the 'Brink of Death.` I have floundered in the 'Sea of Pain.' I was thrashing in the mud of depression and I have been hanging in there barely existing, immersed in fatigue. Now I am alive. I can breathe the air and feel the energy pulsating through my body. I want to leap and yell out to the world that, 'Yes, I am alive again.'"

Dr. Stewart Wong, a sixty-four year old pharmacologist from Washington, D.C., wrote to me describing the wonderful healing benefits he has experienced from the practice of Dr. Chow's Qigong. Since his youth Dr. Wong suffered from severe headaches which usually prevented him from functioning in normal daily activities. On many days he could do little more than get up, wash, eat, and go back to bed. Generally the headaches were relieved only with sleep.

For the next forty years he suffered from a combination of

headaches and nasal congestion from allergies. His only recourse was to treat himself with a series of drugs that did nothing more than suppress his symptoms. In 1993, he attended Dr. Chow's one hour presentation at a major conference. That evening, he witnessed her use of Qigong and acupressure on some of her friends. This was his exposure to Qigong.

He began to practice Qigong. The results surprised him so much he wanted to tell everyone about Qigong. As the first paragraph indicates, his life was turned around by beginning to practice Qigong.

Qigong and Peak Performance

Dr. Chow has given motivational presentations to over 300 corporations, many of them Fortune 500 companies. One program was given for the Prudential Insurance Company in San Francisco in 1987.

Everyone realizes what life must be like for people who sell life insurance. Sales people must continue to find new contacts and make sales presentations. Of 100 such contacts, they are lucky if they sell one life insurance policy. Most people find it difficult to live with such a continual input of negative feed-back.

During the twelve month period following Master Chow's motivational presentation, all sales records were broken. The following statement was made by William Quiring, then General Manager of The Prudential Insurance Co., San Francisco:

A great majority of our people said your (Dr. Chow's) presentation was the best motivational talk they've ever heard. Thank you for helping us find our peak performance. Our San Francisco agency just completed its most successful campaign in history.

Cerebral Palsy

Angela Schuster was born with cerebral palsy. When Dr. Chow

first saw her she was two and one half years old. The following is Bill Good's interview with Angela's mother, Linda, as broadcast on radio station CKNW, Vancouver, British Columbia, in 1992.

Bill Good: Can you give us a brief description of Angela's experience?

Linda: We started seeing Dr. Chow in September (1992). Angela was two years old and moved around by "commando crawling," which means just crawling along on the floor on her elbows. She could not pull herself up. Once she started seeing Dr. Chow, she started pulling herself up. She began to raise her arms and moved around more freely without pain. In the past she didn't want to move because of pain. She couldn't tell us she had pain, but you could see it on her face. With continuing consultations with Dr. Chow, Angela is getting up on her hands and knees on all fours. She's pulling herself up on the coffee table and standing, testing out her balance. All of these improvements have been new and fast.

Good: Were you skeptical in the beginning?

Linda: I was willing to try this treatment and see what it might do...anything that might help Angela. Her father was more skeptical but that soon passed when he saw her improve.

Good: How would you compare the transition in your daughter from a few months ago to today?

Linda: Oh, it's totally like night and day. She's a different little girl.

Good: How have the other doctors and medical staff reacted?

Linda: They're totally amazed, they really are. They don't know what happened; they can't really pinpoint anything, or explain it. I think it's the total combination of all of our work and effort. Angela is a little daredevil now, as far as moving around and everything. She's quite a different child from a year ago.

Dr. Chow said that when she first saw Angela, her legs were so stiff they couldn't be spread apart. She couldn't raise her hands above the level of her shoulders, or walk. She lived in continual pain and cried a great deal.

At the end of the first session Angela was able to raise her hands over head and clap her hands for the first time in her life. That evening she continued to perform this new feat again and again for her parents.

At the end of the third session, she was able to stand and even walked fifty feet with assistance. Walking was most difficult because she didn't have any muscle development in her legs. After this improvement, Dr. Chow met with her physical and occupational therapists, shared ideas, and developed a cooperative approach to Angela's treatment.

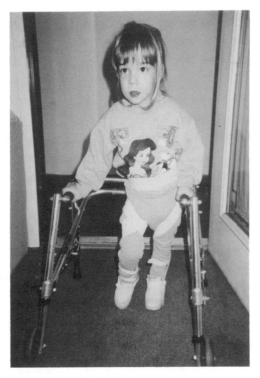

Figure 1: Angela in her walker at age three

Angela is now four years old (May, 1994) and can walk many blocks using a walker with wheels. She goes to school, talks normally, pulls herself up, and can stand by herself for a few moments without assistance. Dr. Chow continues to treat her every time she visits Vancouver, B.C.

Ovarian Cysts, Pre-Menstrual Syndrome, Injured Knee, Chronic Fatigue Syndrome, and Hyperthyroidism

The following is a letter Dr. Chow received from K.K., a housewife and mother of three young boys in Los Angeles,

California.

"I needed a miracle and I found you -- you really have done miracles with my condition, and I am happy.

"I have had a very good life and have a lovely family and home. Since my third pregnancy five years ago, I have been having frequent colds, flu and chest problems. Two years ago, I developed severe pain in my left knee and it made knocking sounds when I moved. I had an MRI (Magnetic Resonance Imagery). My doctor diagnosed it as a probable tear or sprain of the anterior cruciate ligament with fluid in the region of the proximal attachment. There was a possibility that I may need surgery and that was depressing for me. My neck glands also were painful.

"At the same time, I was having a problem with large cysts in my ovaries and also in my throat. I had PMS (Pre-Menstrual Syndrome). One week prior to my period, I would get very hyper, then very depressed when my period began. I had very low energy daily after 2 to 3 P.M. and I usually went to bed early in the evening. Because of the knee pain, I could not bear for my five year old son to sit on my legs for more than a few minutes.

"Our friend, Rick, referred us to you. Because of the distance between Los Angeles and San Francisco, I have had only four sessions with you, and a number of what we call 'telephone Qigong therapies.'

"After the first session on April 24, 1992, my left knee was free of pain for the first time in two years. My neck glands also were free of pain. I felt that I had more energy to 'get up and go'! Psychologically, I felt happier and more hopeful.

"I had my second session the next day, then returned to Los Angeles. I was diligent in practicing what you taught me. This entailed quite a lot of work with breath, posture, body, mind, and spirit (Qigong) exercises. My children found it very entertaining and gleefully giggled as I did my exercises! I persisted and maintained my improvements.

May 2-4: "*I had several parties, stood cooking for two days and there was only a little pain in the knee. On the next day the knee was free of pain. I would not have been able to do any of these things prior to seeing you.*

May 14: "*My period started today; for the first time in five years, it was normal. I did not get severe depression symptoms. I feel calm and have a sense of joy. My energy level is good. The blisters on my tongue are less than half their original size.*

May 18: "*My baby son can sit on my lap for a couple of hours without causing me a lot of discomfort. Before, I could take him only for a few minutes. I had my third session with you today.*

May 27: "*Saw my gynecologist for a pelvic exam and everything checked out normal. All signs of the ovarian cysts have disappeared! I am so happy. The throat blisters are still shrinking.*

June 13: "*I had my fourth session with you. I continue to improve despite the stress of my son breaking his arm. The dandruff and pimples on my scalp also are improving.*

"*In July I had two more telephone Qigong sessions with you, then the last one on August 1st. My doctor checked my knee, said it was normal and no surgery was indicated. There are a number of other minor problems which still need improvement, but I have the hope and encouragement to persist. I continue to progress. When I run into an obstacle, I talk with you. After our conversation I feel better and have a better perspective on things.*

"*I hope that my experience will give others the inspiration to take control of their own health. Miracles do happen. You and your Qigong showed me the way and I am learning to take control of my life again. I know it's all up to me.*"

Neck Pains and Muscle Spasms

Mrs. Loraine Brown suffered a fall (1993) which injured her right ankle and fractured a spinal bone in her neck. Afterward, she lived with continual muscle spasms and numbness of the right hand. Nine months of medical treatments didn't help, and she began to feel helpless and hopeless. She wrote, "I wondered if my seventy-two year old body would shuffle through the remaining years of my life twisted with pain instead of walking freely with confidence. Lifting a light laundry basket, getting out of a car, going up or down steps, getting out of a chair is a continual struggle with pain."

Mrs. Brown happened to hear an audiotape of Dr. Chow's presentation at a major conference, and decided to call for an appointment. She writes, "After a series of six appointments I have experienced a ninety percent improvement in my well being--- physically, mentally, spiritually. I feel that control of my life is in my own hands. My body has returned to health, my mind is at peace, my heart is released to sing."

Victory After a Sports Injury

Robert Jimenez, a competitive skier, injured his knee in early 1986. He was president of the Inland Race Council (skiing), based in San Bernardino, California, and a director of the United States Recreational Skiers Association. During practice runs, prior to competing in the 1987 National Recreational Skiers Championship in Colorado, he re-injured his knee and the pain was so severe he gave up all plans of racing the following morning.

That night Dr. Chow treated him intensively with Qigong for ninety minutes. A rejuvenated Jimenez raced the next morning winning the gold medal in the giant slalom competition by two seconds!

QI MOVES A BALANCE SCALE?

A funny thing happened during our visit to the laboratories of Professor Lu at the Institute of High Energy Physics in Beijing (1990).   As Professor Lu showed us state of the art physics instruments used in his Qigong experiments, we noticed most of the people who had accompanied us were congregated in a corner of the laboratory in front of an ordinary old balanced beam scale.

I had used this type of scale in my college days and it brought back memories of four hour long, boring, laboratory sessions in a quantitative chemistry course. Attorneys like to use drawings of this kind of scale as logos on stationery. When using the scale an object of unknown weight is placed on one side and small calibrated weights are placed on the other until the trays balance evenly. Highly precise measurements can be made which measure to thousandths of a gram. The scale is so sensitive it needs a glass door on its front to isolate the scale from ambient air currents or from the breath of the operator. A locking mechanism controls whether the scale is released for use or locked for protection.

We didn't witness what happened next but we heard the details later from Dr. Kong's chauffeur. The three Qigong masters from Harbin were challenged to see if they could move the scale by telekinesis. Professor Lu's lab attendant closed the door of the scale and released its locking mechanism. The masters tried one by one to move the scale: each failed. They finally tried in unison, emitting their qi at the scale together, off and on, synchronously: one side of the scale tipped. The audience responded with a loud cheer that filled the room, and this was followed by several minutes of chattering in Mandarin.

PATIENCE

The Chinese have a reputation of being patient. In my business dealings with them, I have found them to be anything but patient.

Apparently, in the past, patience was a way of life. One example of patience is the time people devoted to the development of their qi.

Master Taiwu was a hermit who lived on Song Mountain during the Tang Dynasty (618 to 906 AD). Master Taiwu wrote *QiJing, Classic of Qi,* an ancient text describing a method of building up qi through a process of quiet sitting and the swallowing of saliva. He wrote, "The process begins with the cultivation of qi for one year. By the second year the qi will move. By the third, qi will circulate unimpeded." Another quote describing the method was, "Swallowing a thousand times daily is a way to counter aging and revive one's youth." (Source: *Heaven Earth,* a publication of China Advocates, San Francisco.)

Many modern texts about Qigong say similar things. Students are advised that if they practice for one hour a day, they *may* be able to begin to feel their qi within one year. Modern Western people are not going to wait that long for something noticeable to happen! The system described herein usually brings about more rapid progress, but with a high regard for quality of the practice.

Chapter 11: QUESTIONS AND ANSWERS

Q: Dr. Chow: When did you begin to study Qigong?

A: *I would say I have studied Qigong all of my life. As a child I was taught exercises by a neighbor. My intensive study under masters began in the early 1960s, and I continue to study from various masters. This is a lifetime learning process because there is always someone from whom you can learn.*

Q: How much time did you devote to Qigong practice when your studies began?

A: *In the first two or three years, I practiced more intensively, for about one to two hours per day, sometimes more. When I began to work with clients and students I practiced Qigong with them as I taught them. Now, I practice whenever I feel the need, often for about thirty minutes in the morning as soon as I awaken. I also practice at times throughout the day with clients or students.*

Q: How is the ability of one Qigong healer measured and compared with others?

A: *I am not at all certain that Qigong healers should be compared to one another, or if there really is a valid way to compare them. Qigong healers have different capabilities and different foci. Some can speed up bacterial growth, or kill bacteria, some can not. Some can facilitate an immediate movement in people with paralysis, some can not. Some can induce mental improvement, some can not. The best measurement is how patients benefit from the healing attempt, the length of time a healer takes to heal, as well as the longevity of* *the results. Some work only with relatively healthy people.*

Some Qigong healers discover they have special abilities to treat certain disease conditions. After that discovery, many of them like to specialize and try to accept only patients with that condition. Others enjoy seeing patients with a wide assortment of problems.

Q: What do you feel when qi is active in the body?

A: *Qi can be felt in many different ways. It can be felt in the form of heat or a feeling of a quick surge of energy. It might be felt as a tingling sensation, heat or warmth moving slowly through the body with a sense of tranquility, or just a feeling of increased energy. There is a sense of a peacefulness within oneself. Feelings can vary under different circumstances and are related to the situation with which the Qigong master is faced. The palms generally feel warm, or even hot, with a tingling sensation which often is felt most strongly in the hands and finger tips.*

Sometimes a master may feel weightless. Occasionally, he or she may experience that he/she is observing what is going on from above. This is referred to as being in a "Buddha-state of mind." Energy emanations, the colors and intensity of electromagnetism, corona or whatever the term may be, may be seen coming from the body. A master may feel all of these, or none. Someone who is sensitive and can see energy/qi can look at a Qigong master and see an unusually large corona of electromagnetic energy.

Some sensitive people and other healers have said that when they walk into my office they feel this powerful force hitting them and knocking them back. One physician from the East Coast who has been working with the instrumental measurement of energy, reported that when he walked into my office for the first time, he felt a force hit him so strongly he had to retreat and enter again.

Q: From the viewpoint of a Qigong master, what are you doing when you temporarily cause people to lose muscle strength and are able to push even large men around?

A: *It may look as if I am doing something to weaken people, but I am not. I sense the strength and direction their force is moving and breathe with my diaphragm. I combine their force and my own force to direct a powerful action in the direction I want. Breath is all important.*

Q: Can you explain what you are doing when you are treating patients with Qigong?

A: *I become a catalyst for the existing healing qi in the Universe and facilitate the union of the patient to this healing power to ultimately heal himself or herself. When I am with patients, I must do something more. I take protective actions to prevent myself from picking up negative energies that are related to the disease. One of the key ways is to breathe properly. I have a special breath technique that is very effective for re-energizing and replenishing my cells with oxygen.*

Q: What personal satisfaction do you feel from healing a difficult patient?

A: *Most of my clients have been to many other resources and have not been helped, so they often are desperate. Happily, I have been able to help most of them. I am faced almost daily with a life or death situation. Even though these people are alive, they are experiencing a living death and a living hell. When I am able to help, I thank a higher power for the gift I have been given, even though I have worked hard in its development. Still, it is a gift to the extent that I am able to use it effectively. I am very, very thankful for this energy, this qi, that is there for everyone to use. I teach my patients how to use qi. I also teach my clients about the healing process and that they are ultimately the ones who must stimulate their own healing response. It is a very humbling experience, indeed, to know that such power is* *there for all of us to use.*

Q: Is Qigong connected with any religious practice?

A: *No. Qigong was developed under many conditions in China. Some forms developed in Buddhist monasteries, some among physicians and intellectuals.*

The Chinese government investigated Qigong to determine if it was closely linked with any religion or superstition. The conclusion was that Qigong had a scientific basis. If a different conclusion had been reached, Qigong would have been banned by the government and never allowed into the hospital system. People of all religious persuasions can practice Qigong and there is no requirement that any religious beliefs be changed.

Q: You have not described TCM in as much detail as in other books on Qigong. Why?

A: *It was not necessary to do so in this introductory book for the general public. People learn simple systems more easily than ones that are complex. TCM is a large and complicated subject that confuses most Westerners when they hear about its foreign sounding theories for the first time. People want to learn Qigong to maintain health or heal themselves. A simple introduction to TCM will suffice in achieving these goals in the beginning. There is much to learn already if people follow what has been presented. Many excellent texts about TCM are available for those who wish to pursue this fascinating area.*

Q: Can other people learn to do what you do?

A: *Life is energy and energy has unlimited potential. Everyone has the capability to heal or to carry out any and all other phenomena discussed in this book. Some people are fortunate to be born with* *natural abilities, while others must work hard at learning, developing, and bringing out these capabilities. This is similar to learning any other skill. Some people learn easily, others need to study, and work harder before they become proficient.*

Q: What do you teach in your first 100 hour course?

A: *Students learn the basics of body energies, how to do the exercises properly, and work their way through the supportive measures. We practice meditation together with proper posture and breathing. Students, basically, learn more details about what is presented in this introductory book, in addition to other theories of TCM. There are many demonstrations and "hands-on" experiences. Students learn to sense energies with their hands and brush away aches and pains. They also learn twenty-nine techniques in the classical Chinese massage system. The process of working and learning together is of importance.*

Q: What is covered in the second 100 hour course?

A: *In addition to learning more theories and techniques, students learn how to do absentee diagnosis or assessment of an unknown person requiring only the name of the person, birth date, and general vicinity in which he or she lives. From that, along with a special process, they are able to actually visualize or feel the individual and their qi. They learn to sense or see their problems whether physical, emotional or spiritual, and send distant healing to that particular individual. The students have been 95 percent accurate during the active learning and practice period.*

I also teach my students how to visualize the magnetic energy or bio-energy field extending out from the physical human body. The development of these potentials is a tremendous asset for health assessment and healing. Clairvoyancy is a term used for such capabilities.

Q: Is there a third 100 hour training program and, if so, what is taught?

A: *The program contains extensive TCM theories relating to newer concepts of Western energy medicine and psychoneuroimmunology. Students learn more complex techniques of Qigong and the application of Qigong in complex cases. We also have sessions in which students work directly with clients.*

Q: After working with this mysterious thing called the "qi" for so many years, how do you define it now?

A: *We have yet to determine the true nature of qi. There are many theories about qi but many are inconsistent. I respect qi as a powerful and special phenomenon that, for a lack of a better term, is generally described as energy. Miracles brought about through Qigong can be said to occur because of a shift of qi, and must be looked at seriously with great respect. Qi is the vital essence of life itself.*

Q: Are some people born with natural healing abilities?

A: *There is no doubt about this. In China, we were told that the aging leader, Deng Xiao Ping, and many other leaders, receive daily treatments to build up and balance their energies. The man who treats Deng was born with these gifts and never studied any system or method of energy work.*

Q: Are "psychic abilities" associated with Qigong?

A: *Paranormal phenomena might be considered to be a remote branch of Qigong. Some high level masters have demonstrated these abilities, others have not.*

Q: Have any Qigong masters tried to use their unusual abilities to harm people?

A: *In China Dr. Kong told us this apparently has happened. A Qigong master used his special abilities to play pranks on people he did not like. Suddenly he lost his "powers" as if they had been taken away by a higher power.*

APPENDIX I: PHYSIOTHERAPY NOTES ON ERIC (AGE 8) DESCRIBED IN CHAPTER 1 (unedited)

BEFORE FIRST SESSION WITH DR. CHOW:

History of hand function: "Flexion ulnar deviation pattern of hand when trying to grasp. Unable to extend at MP joints when wrist is in flexion. Unable to achieve pincer grip. Thumb hyperextends at DIP joint, flexes and adducts (to move in the direction of the center line of the body) at MP and PIP joints. Holds arm in abnormal pronation (movement away from the center line of the body) to do a raking type of grasp."

Leg Function: "On attempted dorsi flexion (flexing the foot up toward the head), the foot exerts, toes extend, with minimal evidence of any active dorsi flexion. 5 to 10 degrees passive dorsi flexion. Left foot adducted, walks on toes of left foot, unable to dorsi flex the foot to clear the floor. Incapable of doing a heel toe gait with left foot flat on floor. Incapable of doing heel toe gait with left foot. Exhibits associated retraction and flexion of left arm with wrist and finger flexion, exaggerated when he tries to walk faster. When he runs he hits the floor with his metatarsal heads which sets off a strong extensor thrust and he cannot get his heel to the floor: he is thrown forward by the extensor thrust (when attempting to run he falls flat on his face)."

AFTER FIRST TWO TREATMENTS BY DR. CHOW

"Eric was able to pick up using finger to thumb in slightly inferior pincer grip. Was able to oppose thumb to finger, flexing the thumb appropriately. When Dr. Chow worked on his leg, he voluntarily extended his wrist and took his weight on an extended hand with shoulder externally rotated. This is not a position which I have seen him voluntarily assume. Eric was able to hold his foot at a 90 degree angle. Able to walk with a flat foot at a slow pace and then at a faster pace. There was no associated reaction in the arm whatsoever, even when the pace was picked up. He was able to do almost a complete deep knee bend with both heels flat on the floor. He was able to do high step, with toes hitting the floor first, and then coming down onto the heel without falling forward."

REPORT OF AUGUST 1987 SESSION WITH DR. CHOW, BEFORE TREATMENT

"In this August session, it was observed that Eric maintained his ability to come down on the heels when standing, walking, or running, but required frequent reminders to do so. He had lost some of his ability for thumb-finger opposition due to lack of practice. He was having therapy only once in two weeks which is inadequate, and the doctors are still recommending another heel cord operation."

AFTER TREATMENT

"Eric was able to pick up object with good finger-thumb opposition. Wrist showed more active extension to stabilize it. Ankle movement was much freer in all directions, with slightly more than 90 degrees of active dorsiflexion achieved. Able to maintain heel on floor better. Could stand and balance on each leg for a short time. Holding furniture lightly he could use both the right and the left foot to kick a cloth ball with good balance and return the kicking foot to an exact position right next to the other foot. He was also able to spontaneously let go of the furniture support on a couple of occasions and maintain the quality of movement. Motivation to concentrate is to be a better ball player than the other boys."

APPENDIX II: RESOURCES

The reader should understand that there are relatively few people outside of China who currently are knowledgeable about Qigong. Qigong masters usually can be found in large urban centers such as London, San Francisco, and New York. Most masters teach Qigong, and some also practice healing. At present, there is no certification process so, before deciding to see a given Qigong master, you should find out as much about the master as you can, search out recommendations and take your time. Obviously some Qigong masters are better than others.

The resources in this section are presented as a guide so the reader will be able to receive more information about Qigong in a given region. To the best of our knowledge, the information is accurate, but it is not intended to be comprehensive. Please be advised that we can not be responsible for the actions of others.

ORGANIZATIONS IN THE UNITED STATES

California

China Advocates, 1635 Irving Street, San Francisco, CA 94122. 415-665-4505. Contact: Howard Dewar. Offers specialized tours to China in a variety of subjects, including Qigong.

China Healthways Institute, 117 Avenida Granada, San Clemente, CA 92672. Tel. 800-743-5608. Distributors of the "Qigong Machine"

Health Action, 19 East Mission #102, Santa Barbara, CA 93101, Offers audiotapes and books, as well as training programs for the public and future teachers of Qigong. Chief of Staff Roger Jahnke,

OMD, is available for public lectures. Tel. 805-682-3230. Fax 805-569-5832.

Institute of Noetic Sciences, P.O. Box 909, Sausalito, CA 94966. 415-331-5650. Contact person: Marilyn Schlitz.

The Qigong Institute, East West Academy of Healing Arts, 450 Sutter St., Suite 2104, San Francisco, CA 94108 Phone: 415-788-2227. Fax: 415-788-2242. Contact: Master Effie Poy Yew Chow, or Dr. Kenneth Sancier. Offers courses in Qigong from Dr. Chow and other practitioners, personal consultations with Dr. Chow, membership, international networking, data base, tapes, videos, scientific references, scientific meetings, and other Qigong related materials. e-mail: eastwest@infinex.com
http://web.idirect.com/~qigong

Qi Gong Resource Associates, 1755 Homet Road, Pasadena, CA 91106. 818-564-9751. Contact: Shantika Lamanno, who is available for public lectures.

Wong, Chung Siu, Doctor of TCM, Qigong master and North American Representative of the Guo Lin Research Society, 940 Washington St., San Francisco, CA 94108. Tel: 415-788-1008.

World Research Foundation, 15300 Ventura Blvd., Suite 405, Sherman Oaks, CA 91403. 818-907-5483. Offers Qigong video tapes and books, as well as information about other alternative medicine therapies.

Colorado

Chi Kung and Corporate Training Associates, P.O. Box 2677, Aspen, CO 81612. 303-945-4050. Training programs for corporate executives in the United States and Europe.

Hawaii

The East West Center, University of Hawaii at Manoa, School of Medicine, Honolulu, HI 96822.

Idaho

Genesee Valley Daoist Hermitage, Box 9224, Moscow, ID 83843. Offers study in Daoist philosophy, Qigong, meditation, Chang Ming nutrition, and residential study in China. No phone listing.

Massachusetts

Yang's Martial Arts Association, 38 Hyde Park Ave., Jamaica Plains, MA 02130-4132. 617-524-8892. Fax 617-524-4184.

The Boston Study Group of East/West Life Science/Technology, 17 Sunset Road, Winchester, MA 01890.

New York

The Healing Tao, The Immortal Tao Foundation, P.O. Box 1194, Huntington, NY 11743. 516-367-2701. Fax 516-367-2754. Workshops and trainings are held internationally.

International College of Acupuncture and Electro-therapeutics, 800 Riverside Drive (8-I), New York, NY 10032. 212-781-6262. Contact: Yoshiaki Omura, M.D., Sc.D.

United Nations Staff Research Group, Room S-2311, United Nations, P.O. Box 20, Grand Central Station, New York, NY 10017. Contact person: Ching Huang Lin.

Ohio

Qigong Academy, 8103 Marlborough Ave., Cleveland, OH 44129. 216-842-9628. Offers instruction in Qigong. Contact: Richard Leirer.

Qigong Human Life Research Foundation, P.O. Box 5327, Cleveland, OH 44101. Offers courses and a quarterly newsletter about Qigong, in addition to two classes at Case Western University Medical School. Phone: 216-475-4712. Contact: Master Tian You Hao.

Tennessee

Chinese National Chi Kung Institute, 2068 Sunnyside Dr., Brentwood TN. Tel. 615-370-8992. Fax. 615-371-8990. Orders only 1-800-566-5586. Offers a variety of Qigong courses both locally and by mail. Video instruction tapes are also available.

Washington

QiWay: Mind, Body, Spirit and Energy Medicine, 2814 S. Grand, Spokane, Washington, 99203. Phone 509-747-0877 or 1-800 Rx QiWay. Offers Chow Qigong, workshops, classes and other seminars. Contact Linda Chiu Hole, M.D.

Washington, D.C.

US-China Peoples Friendship Association, 2025 Eye Street N.W., Suite 715, Washington, D.C. 20006. 202-296-4147.

INTERNATIONAL ORGANIZATIONS

Australia

Qigong Association of Australia, 458 White Horse Road, Surrey Hills, Victoria 3127. 03-836-6961. Contact: Master Jack Lim.

Canada

East West Academy of Healing Arts, Toronto. Tel: (416) 920-4008, or (415) 788-2227 (in San Francisco.) Fax:(416) 921-2268.

East West Academy of Healing Arts Society, Vancouver, B.C. Tel: (604) 739-4284 or (415) 788-2227 in San Francisco. Fax: (415) 788-2242. e-mail: eastwest@infinex.com http://web.idirect.com/~qigong

Shou-Yu Liang Wushu Institute, 7951 No. 4 Road, Richmond, B.C., Canada V6Y 2T4. 604-228-3604. 604-273-9648.

World Natural Medical Foundation, 9904-106 Street, Edmonton, Alberta, Canada T5K 1C4. Phone 403-426-2760. Fax: 403-426-5650. Contact: Steven K. H. Aung, M.D.

China

The International Qigong Science Association, c/o Prof. Wang, Qi-Ping, Somatic Science Research Center Dept. of Electrical Engineering, Xan Jiao Tong University, Xian, Shaanxi Provence, China 710049.

The World Academic Society of Medical Qigong, c/o Mr. Hua Yuan, He Ping Jie Beikou, Bei San Huan Lu 29, Beijing 100013, China.

China Wushu Association, #3 An-Din Road, Chao-Yang District, Beijing, China 100101. 491-2150.

Qigong Master Liu Hengshun can be contacted at: Building No. 12-4-603, Shuangyushu Dongli, Haidian District, Beijing, China 100086. Tel. 86-1-255-6996.

AUDIO AND VIDEOTAPES

Audio: Chow Integrated Healing System Meditation Tape. Available through the East West Academy of Healing Arts, 450 Sutter St. #2104, San Francisco, CA 94108, Tel. 415-788-2227, or MediPress, PO Box 5154, Coeur d'Alene, ID 83814. Orders 1-800-775-5300. Price: $12.95 plus $3.50 shipping (U.S.).

Video: Chow Integrated Healing System Qigong Exercises, a tape of exercises illustrated in Chapter 7 in motion with instruction. For information contact the East West Academy of Healing Arts, 450 Sutter St. #2104, San Francisco, CA 94108, Tel. 415-788-2227, or MediPress, PO Box 5154, Coeur d' Alene, ID 83814. Orders 1-800-775-5300. Price: $40.00 plus $3.50 shipping (U.S.)

MAGAZINES AND CATALOGUES

INTERNAL ARTS CATALOG, P.O. Box 1777, Arlington, Texas 76004. Publisher: Dr. John P. Painter. 1-800-223-6984. Fax 817-460-5125.

KUNG FU/QIGONG MAGAZINE, Pacific Rim Publishers, 3500 Thomas Rd. Bldg. G, Santa Clara, California 95054. Tel 1-800 Tai Chee.

QI - THE JOURNAL OF TRADITIONAL EASTERN HEALTH AND FITNESS, Inside graphics Inc., Box 221343, Chantilly, VA 22022. Publisher: Steve Rhodes. 703-378-3859. Fax 703-378-0663.

QIGONG MEDICAL SCIENCE, a discussion and analysis of selected scientific papers, which were presented at the Third International Qigong Symposium, Shanghai, China, 1990, that report

statistically significant effects of qi on different kinds of living systems. Available Through the Qigong Institute, East West Academy of Healing Arts, 450 Sutter St. #2104. San Francisco, CA, 94108. 415-788-2227, Fax 415-788-2242.

A long list of publications, scientific papers, abstracts of meetings on Qigong in China and elsewhere is available through the Qigong Institute, including the following:

1. PROCEEDINGS OF THE FIRST WORLD CONFERENCE FOR ACADEMIC EXCHANGE OF MEDICAL QIGONG, Beijing, China, 1988. Abstracts in English available through the Qigong Institute, East West Academy of Healing Arts, 450 Sutter St, #2104, San Francisco, CA 94108. Telephone 415-788-2227

2. PROCEEDINGS OF THE SECOND INTERNATIONAL CONFERENCE ON QIGONG, September 10-15, 1989, Xian China. Abstracts in English available Through the Qigong Institute, East West Academy of Healing Arts, as above.

3. PROCEEDINGS OF THE THIRD INTERNATIONAL SYMPOSIUM ON QIGONG, Sept 17-20, 1990, Shanghai, China. Abstracts in English available through Qigong Institute, East West Academy of Healing Arts, as above.

4. PROCEEDINGS OF THE SECOND WORLD CONFERENCE

FOR MEDICAL QIGONG, September, 1993, Beijing, China. Abstracts in English available through the Qigong Institute, East West Academy of Healing Arts, as above.

REDWING REVIEWS, Redwing Book Company, 44 Linden St., Brookline, Massachusetts 02146. Publisher: Bob Felt. 1-800-873-3946 Fax 617-738-4620.

THE WONDERS OF QIGONG, A CHINESE EXERCISE FOR FITNESS, HEALTH AND LONGEVITY, China Sports Magazine 01985, Published by Wayfarer Publications, P.O. Box 26156, Los Angeles, CA 90026.

T'AICHI, Wayfare Publications, Box 26156, Los Angeles, CA 90026. Publisher: Marvin Smalheiser. 213-665-7773. Fax 213-665-1627.

EQUIPMENT

The "Qigong Machine," a light-weight portable machine that emits low frequency energy which is reported to be modeled after the qi emitted by Qigong masters, and reported to have therapeutic value. For more information a brochure describing its benefits is available through the Qigong Institute, East West Academy of Healing Arts, 450 Sutter St. #2104, San Francisco, CA 94108.

APPENDIX III: A SUMMARY OF THE CHOW SYSTEM

Components Used By Everyone

Proper posture in standing/walking/sitting
Proper breathing with the diaphragm
Meditation
Proper diet and food preparation
Vitamin and mineral supplements
Qigong exercises---live the qi concept
Hugs---at least eight daily
Laughter---at least three belly laughs daily
Positive mental attitudes
Listing fantasies
Listing goals and dreams
Positive attitudes of self and friends
Prioritizing time for yourself
Positive affirmations and the computer-mind
Be at peace with self and others---conflict resolution
Handling secrets with friends
Partner in healing
Lifestyle changes
The child in us as a whole; each part of us is a child
TCM principles

Optional Components Used as Indicated

Drawings
Art
Music

Performing arts
Acupressure

Components Used by Qigong Master Chow to Supplement The Above

TCM diagnostic measures
Counselling
Stress management skills
Emission of qi - Qigong
Herbs
Qigong acupressure
Moxibustion
Cupping
Classical Chinese massage, tuinah, ahnmoh
Feng Shui
Acupuncture
Others

For people just beginning to learn this system, the most important introductory components are listed below:

1) At least eight hugs a day
2) At least three belly laughs a day
3) A positive mental attitude
4) Proper posture and breathing with the diaphragm
5) Meditation daily
6) Good nutrition, supplements, perhaps herbs
7) Qigong exercises
8) Be at peace with yourself and others
9) Live the qi energy concept
10) Give and receive lots of love

BIBLIOGRAPHY

Blofeld, John, *Taoism, The Quest for Immortality*, London, Unwin Paperbacks, 1979.

Chang, Stephen T., *The Book of Internal Exercises*, San Francisco, California, Strawberry Hill Press, 1978.

Chia, Mantak, has written a collection of Qigong related books including *Chi Self Massage; Iron Shirt Chi Kung; Bone Marrow Nei Kung; Taoist Secrets of Love; Cultivating Male Sexual Energy;* Published in New York by Aurora Press.

Chen, Xinnong, *Chinese Acupuncture and Moxibustion*, Beijing, China, Foreign Languages Press, 1990.

Chungliang, Al Huang, *Embrace Tiger Return to Mountain: The Essence of Taiji,* Celestial Arts.

Connelly, Diane M., *Traditional Acupuncture: The Law of the Five Elements,* Columbia, Maryland, 1979.

Connor, Danny, *Qigong*, York Beach, Maine, Samuel Weiser, Inc., 1992.

Dong, Paul, *The Four Major Mysteries of Mainland China,* Englewood Cliffs; Prentice Hall, 1984.

Dong, Paul, and Esser, Aristide, *Chi Gong: The Ancient Chinese* Way *to Health,* New York, Paragon House, 1990.

Eisenberg, David, *Encounters with Qi; Exploring Chinese Medicine,* New York, Viking Penguin, 1985.

Jiao, Guorui, *Qigong, Essentials for Health Promotion*, Beijing, China Reconstructs Press, 1988.

Jwing-Ming, Yang, *The Root of Chinese Chi Kung, the Secrets of Chi Kung Training*, Massachusetts, Jamaica Plain, 1989.

Kaptchuk, Ted, *The Web That Has No Weaver*, New York, Congdon & Weed, 1983. Described by many people as the best introductory book on TCM written by a Westerner.

Lao Tzu, *Tao Te Ching: The Book of Perfectibility*, London, Concord Grove Press, 1983.

MacRitchie, James, *Chi Kung, Cultivating Personal Energy*, Rockport, MA, Element, Inc., 1993.

Siou, Lily, *Chi Kung The Art of Mastering the Unseen Life Force*, Rutland, Vermont, Charles E. Tuttle Co, 1975.

Takahashi, Masaru, and Brown, Stephen, *Chinese Qigong for Health, Traditional Exercises for Cure and Prevention*, Tokyo and New York, Japan Publications, Inc., 1986.

Temple, Robert, *The Genius of China: 3,000 Years of Science, Discovery, and Invention*. New York, Simon and Schuster, 1986.

Veith, I., trans. *The Yellow Emperor's Classic of Internal Medicine*. 2nd ed. Berkeley, California, University of California Press, 1972.

Zhang, Enquin, Ed., *Basic Theory of Traditional Chinese Medicine*, Volumes I and II, Shanghai, China. Publishing House of Shanghai College of Traditional Chinese Medicine, 1990. (530 Lingling Road)

Zhang, Enquin, Ed., *Chinese Acupuncture and Moxibustion*, Shanghai, China. Publishing House of Shanghai College of Traditional Chinese Medicine, 1990.

Zhang, Enquin, Ed., Shanghai, China. *Prescriptions of Chinese Medicine*, Shanghai, China. Publishing House of Shanghai College of Traditional Chinese Medicine, 1990.

Zhang, Enquin, Ed., *Chinese Materia Medica,* Shanghai, China. Shanghai College of Traditional Chinese Medicine, 1990.

Zhang, Enquin, Ed., *Health Preservation and Rehabilitation,* Shanghai, China. Shanghai College of Traditional Chinese Medicine, 1990.

Zhang, Enquin, Ed., *Chinese Medicated Diet,* Shanghai, China. Shanghai College of Traditional Chinese Medicine, 1990.

Zhang, Minguu, et. al., *Chinese Qigong Therapy,* Jinan, China, Shandong Science and Technology Press, 1985.

GLOSSARY

Acupuncture: The use of needles to stimulate energy points.

Dantian: or Seat of Life, located two inches below navel and one inch inward where qi is stored.

Daoism (Taoism): To live the right way in balance with nature.

Doctor of Traditional Chinese Medicine: A physician in China who has completed training in a traditional Chinese medical school.

Energy Points: A series of over 600 points on the skin which, when stimulated, can affect the energy system in the body.

Guo Lin Qigong: A style of Qigong developed by Qigong Master Guo Lin; used to treat cancer.

Hard Qigong: A martial arts form of Qigong.

Kirlian Photography: A system of high voltage photography that can demonstrate changes in energy balance.

Master: A person who has achieved the highest level of achievement.

Meridian System (energy system): a system of twelve bilateral energy pathways (and others) through the body.

Microcosmic Orbit: The circulation of energy through the Conception Vessel (midline of front of body) and Governing Vessel (midline of the back of the body).

Moxa: Stimulation of an energy point with deep heat using the herb artemisia vulgaris.

Pulse Diagnosis: The taking of six superficial and six deep pulses on the radial artery at each wrist to detect the status of health.

Qigong Doctor: A person who has had training to treat people with qi.

Soft Qigong: Medical, or healing Qigong.

Table of Correspondences: correlation of things (ie. colors, sounds, tastes) related to The Law of the Five Elements.

Taiji (Tai Chi): A movement form of Qigong.

Touch Healing: A Western term for healing with the hands.

Wei Qi: Energy that is being transmitted from the body.

Yin and Yang: The dual forces, positive and negative components of all nature.

ABOUT THE AUTHORS

Charles T. McGee, M.D., has worked for Project HOPE treating primitive life style Indians in Ecuador and for the Center for Disease Control in Atlanta, Georgia. He began to study acupuncture after a trip to the far East in 1974. These experiences led him to study TCM, as well as to give up the practice of obstetrics in favor of an alternative medicine practice.

In 1987 a Chinese governmental official asked him to become a consultant to innovative health programs, and this led to a series of trips to China. While in China his host literally pushed him into Qigong, which since has become his center of interest.

Dr. Chow has a Ph.D. in higher education and a masters degree in behavioral sciences and communications. She is a registered nurse and holds a diploma in public health and psychiatric nursing. She is also a Qigong master, a national diplomate (NCAA), and California licensed acupuncturist. She has been teaching and using Qigong in a Traditional Chinese Medicine practice for over thirty years, and is the most prominent proponent of Qigong outside of China.

Dr. Chow has been the recipient of many awards, including the "Presidents Citation Award" of the American Association for Acupuncture and Oriental Medicine, Distinguished Award from the National Society for Acupuncturists of the Republic of China, an award from the Ministry of Health, Department of Occupational Health, Republic of China, an award from the Medical Services of the National Army of the Republic of China, the American Nurses Association Award for Women's Honors in Public Service Awards in Entrepreneurship, the Outstanding Service award towards the recognition, advancement and acceptance of the Science of Acupuncture in the U.S. (from the National Acupuncture Association), and the "Woman Warrior Award" for contributions to the Health Field from the Pacific Asian American Women's Bay Area Coalition. In June of 1994 she received honored recognition by the Ethnic/Racial Minority Fellowship Programs of the American Nurses Association. She also is listed in Women's Who's Who of the World.

Recently she was appointed to the Editorial Advisory Board of Rodale Press for a special publication on alternative medicine, and the Editorial Advisory Board of the Journal of Alternative and Complementary Medicine. In the past twenty years she personally has presented to over 200,000 people of all cultures, more than 350 business corporations, including Fortune 500 Companies, hospitals, health clinics, and universities. She has made many radio and television appearances both in North America and Europe, including multiple appearances on the Gary Collins show.

INDEX

RESOURCE REQUEST FORM

NAME:_____

ADDRESS:_____

CITY:_____ ST:_____ ZIP:_____

PHONE: (H)_____ (W)_____

OCCUPATION:_____

I AM INTERESTED IN THE FOLLOWING:

☐ I would like information about the Qigong Institute/East West Academy of Healing Arts.

☐ I would like to take training in The Chow System.

☐ I would like to help organize a seminar/training program in my area.

☐ I would like a private consultation with Dr. Chow.

☐ Dr. Chow's Meditation tape. ($12.95) $_____

☐ Dr. Chow's Videotape on Qigong Exercises ($40.00) $_____

Shipping: (U.S. and Canada) $ 3.50

Total: **$** _____

☐ VISA   ☐ M/C   ☐ CHECK

CC#:_____
EXP. DATE:_____
SIGNATURE:_____

PLEASE MAKE CHECKS PAYABLE TO MEDIPRESS
PO BOX 5154, COEUR D' ALENE, ID 83814
OR CALL 1-800-775-5300

September, 1998

Many people have written us to tell of the exceptional health benefits they experienced from following the book and tapes - with no other instruction:

"I am in top health now because of Dr. Chow's book. My three years of chronic fatigue caused me to stop work and school. I was home-bound for four months before I found the book. I practiced 3-4 hours each day for three months and my life completely turned around. Now I am in top shape, work full-time, went to school full-time and got my Bachelor's degree. I hike, bike, dance, volunteer and sing with vigor."

"My father's angina pains were relieved."
"My schizophrenic mind and body feels so much better."
"I have more energy and stamina."
"I can sleep better"
"I don't need as much sleep."
"I am not as stressed out as I have been."
"I had to wear glasses because of cataracts and was scheduled for eye surgery. After following your book, I can read without my glasses. The physician canceled my surgery."

"My nurse/client who had been on disability for seven years due to chronic fatigue syndrome wrote after one week of following the book that her "life has been turned around" and she will be going back to work. As her physician I had given her the book to read and now am giving the book to other patients to follow."

"My cousin had two operations for his brain tumor, was scheduled for a third with questionable chances. The operation was canceled because the tumor shrank after Chow Qigong"

RESOURCE REQUEST FORM

NAME:_____

ADDRESS:_____

CITY:_____ ST:_____ ZIP:_____

PHONE: (H)_____ (W)_____

OCCUPATION:_____

I AM INTERESTED IN THE FOLLOWING:

☐ I would like information about the Qigong Institute/East West Academy of Healing Arts.

☐ I would like to take training in The Chow System.

☐ I would like to help organize a seminar/training program in my area.

☐ I would like a private consultation with Dr. Chow.

☐ Dr. Chow's Meditation tape. ($12.95) $_____

☐ Dr. Chow's Videotape on Qigong Exercises $_____
   ($40.00)

            Shipping: (U.S. and Canada) $ 3.50

                                Total: **$** _____

      ☐ VISA   ☐ M/C   ☐ CHECK

CC#:_____

EXP. DATE:_____

SIGNATURE:_____

PLEASE MAKE CHECKS PAYABLE TO MEDIPRESS
PO BOX 5154, COEUR D' ALENE, ID 83814
OR CALL 1-800-775-5300

This book was written to be simple, but not simplistic, intended for people who are in areas where there is no Qigong teacher, or there are teachers of other styles. Simple so that first -time readers foreign to the idea of Qi could grasp the hope of Qigong to benefit them whoever they are and in whatever status of health they are.

Qigong brings a more exuberant, exhilarating, positive, and healthier life from the standpoint of body, mind, and spirit, and connects us to the nature of the universe. Whether you are super healthy, like the Olympic competitor, or you are a top executive, clerk, teacher, caregiver, professional, child or student or whoever-- Chow Qigong is for you. The book was written so that you can pick it up and follow your own development in Qigong step by step. If you only have a few minutes, or if you have hours per day, Qigong has proven to be successful.

Hundreds of readers like the above have called or written after they read the book and followed it, and told of the significant benefits. Some of these people have continued to practice Chow Qigong on their own with the book and the videos and with intermittent consultations with Dr. Chow by telephone.

Others have joined us physically on our more vigorous training programs. Some have gone on to teach the Chow Qigong exercises and meditation, and some have developed the Chow Qigong community in their area. Others have developed an educational practice in which they see people individually, and have helped many with minor to serious conditions such as respiratory conditions, pain, RSI, heart conditions, and even cancer.

We hope that you will get equally excited and enthused about Chow Qigong and reap its benefits. We would appreciate hearing from you as we did from these people. E-mail us at eastwestqi@aol.com or fax us at (415)788-2242. Be sure to keep in touch through our Web site: http://www.eastwestqi.com

Wishing you good health and good Qi!